The Aut

Annie Christina Knox was born in 1937 in County Mayo, Eire and from 1940 - 1955 lived in Coventry where she received her education.

She studied History at Manchester University and trained there as a teacher.

Her life was occupied with bringing up her five children whilst following a career as a teacher, working for 40 years in Lancashire and Hampshire, finally returning to her formative neighbourhood in Coventry.

At this time, she contrived to follow further studies in the Philosophy of Education, Child Psychotherapy, and Divinity.

After retirement, at 68 years, she became a children's catechist at Our Lady of Assumption Church in Coventry and composed this memoir.

She continues to contribute with pride to family, church and community.

Chrissie O'

The Story of a Catholic, Irish, Immigrant, Child

For My Children, Elizabeth, Peter, James, Fiona and Liam,
and my grandchildren, Cheyney, Adam, Joe, Ollie,
Anna, Ellie, Edward, Stephanie, Joe and Kane, and my
great-grandchild Liam
with love.

CONTENTS

Prologue

Chapters

1. Origins
 – "County Mayo, God Help Us!"   1937-1939

2. Journey and Arrival
 – "If You Ever Go Across the Sea to England....."   1939

3. The Blitz
 – "From the Bogs to the Bombs"   1941

4. Another Household
 – "Life in a Court – Dickensian Style!"   1941-1942

5. Evacuation
 – "Cut to the Quick – and Not Just the Nails."

6. Vincent Street
 – "New Home, New Hope, Old Terrors"

7. Scarlet Fever
 – "Death Comes Stalking Once Again"

8. The Beginning of the End of the War
 – "Got any gum Chum?"   1942-1945

9. Early School Days
 – "Saint Ossie's at Last – Hurrah!"   1943-1946

10. Holy Communion and the Arrival of Baby Teresa
 – "I Once had a Sweet Little Doll Dears"   1944

11. Passion for the Written Word
 – "Realms of Gold"   1944-1946

Chapters

12. Conflicts with John and Helen
– "A bedbug would wake her walking past on the pillow."

13. Household Routines
– An Hour's Queue for Half a Pound of Sausages

14. Up The Top
– "Children Rule – OKAY?"

15. Back to Education
– "Not Fat Henry VIII Again!"

16. The Scholarship
– "In Search of the Holy Grail"

17. Interim
– "What a Feckin' Winter!"

18. Waiting……. Waiting.
– "Like Flies on the Flank of a Whale"   1948

19. Waiting…… Waiting.
– "Only a sweet and virtuous soul,"

20. The Scholarship Results
– "Well worth the sacrifice of chips"

21. Barr's Hill Grammar School for Girls
– "Arduus ad Astra"

22. Alienation
– "Where do I belong"

23. Coda

Epilogue – My Journey in Poems

Acknowledgements

Prologue

In my late seventies, looking back to my childhood years, I became increasingly aware of many inherent themes of that time which were of considerable significance and relevance in today's world. They were certainly worthy of recording and capturing. Those years of childhood in my understanding, spanned from birth to the age of twelve, 1937-1950.

Of importance was the theme of immigration. It was in my case the transition from a simple rural, farming-peasant lifestyle in the West of Ireland to the increasingly industrialised, urban environment of the City of Coventry in the Midlands of England. The former lifestyle was dominated by a strong religious ethos with close ties to agriculture and the land; the latter was much more secular in character. Irish labour was needed and was advertised for by the burgeoning car factories of Coventry and a particularly fertile source of manpower was the impoverished west coast of Ireland, in our case, County Mayo. Fifteen years before the Windrush generation England was accepting diversity of cultures and beliefs in the interest of economic progress.

An even more dramatic and a pivotal historical theme was the that of life in wartime. World War II began in 1939, the year my mother arrived in England to join her husband, with her three young children, and it was soon after, in 1940, that Hitler's aggression began strongly to target the cities of England. Coventry, because of the dominance of munitions producing factories received some of the heaviest attacks of the war. The word "Coventrate" emerged as a verb to describe the effects of a particularly devastating and destructive air raid. Revisiting those times of wartime ordeals I felt that it was of value to recreate in writing the first hand experiences of families such as ours, who suffered the privations of bombing and blitz, of deaths and injury, of shelters and blackouts, of evacuation and rationing, of blasted houses and endless rehousing – and of so many more painful experiences that are daunting to remember, impossible to forget and certainly worthy of recall.

Alongside these two important themes I felt that my family in particular had a personal tale to tell in so far as it grew from three children in 1937 to eight children in 1950. By 1955 it had grown to twelve but those years are outside the remit of my story. The narration of family life, and its struggles with nutrition, hygiene, heating, discipline, and what was a priority with my parents, the careful upbringing of their children in a devout and caring Catholic faith, with always the conviction above all, in God's love – all these things seemed momentous to me and should be shared.

The tale of family life too is made more interesting because my parents, like many other immigrants were virtually orphans in a foreign land. The majority of their families had already emigrated to the United States and very few remained in Ireland, (one in a convent). The story of their deprivation inevitably had its influence on family life – not least when an unknown young American soldier arrived at our house in the blackout of a dangerous night to introduce himself to my mother as her brother Michael, born in Philadelphia! Now as a bomber pilot he was helping to rescue us from a terrible defeat, by the Germans.

Family life, then, has a great sociological interest. For me personally though I felt it was the inner life of the child that needed expression. I was probably lucky that I always had had a very vivid memory and a period of psychoanalysis in my late forties probably reactivated many early experiences and memories which I could capture in this memoir. I was also so lucky that my mother talked so openly and intelligently about emotions and events, relationships and difficulties. I sometimes felt that the richness of our communications was in part due to the gaping absence in her own life of mother and father and brother and sister and that in some way the companionship of her daughters, Helen and me in particular, helped her to make sense of life.

It is probably the introspective story in this memoir that is most important. This child is very conscious of an inner spiritual life and as she grows, longs for intellectual development and education. Inevitably the memoir deals with war-time schooling with all its limitations but also reveals the emotional upheavals accompanying the Scholarship system and the challenges of Grammar school for children of immigrant status. It touches too on the sheer wonder and delight of learning but in complete contrast captures the existence of the most lively and rich childhood culture that dominated poor areas that gave an independence, sociability and creativity to life that now for children seems so sadly missing. Very briefly at the end of the memoir the problems and pains of identity are alluded to.

    I know the anecdotal style of a memoir raises often questions for the reader, just as it raised many questions for the writer. But I hope you enjoy reading and find admiration for some of the characters you encounter, most particularly my mother and my father.

1
Origins
"County Mayo, God Help Us!"

I was a Catholic, Irish child before I was an immigrant – at least for two and a half years I was. Three miles from the one-road town of Kiltimagh, amidst bleak fields, in the county of Mayo, on the far west coast of Ireland, there stood

in 1937 (and still stands today – though home to hay for cows, and not to people) a little stone cottage with living room warmed by a great turf fire and beyond, through a narrow opening, a bedroom for a bed. and in that bed, beneath a cracked window, I was born.

"An easy birth," my mother told me, and I can imagine her fair, pink skin, beaded with sweat, and all her thick, coppery, hair curling damply on the pillow. "Or maybe it was easy," she said, "because I had John in the bed beside me, gasping for breath with the asthma, and the wind blowing fierce through that crack in the window. I had hardly time to think you were coming." It wasn't a complaint. It was a statement of fact.

After all, it was October in that bleak, isolated place near the Atlantic coast, a tiny cottage set within twenty eight acres of rocky land, ("my nearest neighbour", she told me, was two fields away and the river to cross). Her husband John was away working in the fast-growing city of Coventry, in England. She had also care of her children, John Patrick aged 3 and 2 year old Helen. Yet, in spite of all this, something tells me that I was greatly welcome, the fruit of a special love, (conceived perhaps on a Christmas trip home by my dad, on one of those infrequent marital unions). In my bones to this day I have a certain knowledge of a warm welcome to this world, to this soft, pretty, brave mother of only five and twenty years, amidst the barren fields of Mayo. I was the baby with auburn hair like hers, (but never so rich in hue nor so full of curl) and this, after the first two born in the O'Brien family were dark-haired like my father, John. I was to be given, in baptism, in the stately church of Kiltimagh, on the day after my birth, her own name, Annie, but with Christina as a second name, different from hers, which was Celia.

God knows we were not rich. The tiny house was sparse, with few possessions. It was that same house where my mother had grown up under the care of her uncle Pat and Auntie Annie. The most prized possessions there were the two holy pictures, "Jesus walking on the Waters" and

"Our Lady of the Sacred Heart". These same pictures were the ones that my mother wrapped in newspaper and brought with her to England, when two and a half years later, in the year 1940, she left with us three children to join my dad in Coventry.

Did she know there was a war on? Did she know Coventry was to be a prime target of Hitler? Did she know that Coventry was, only a year later, to be Coventrated? Probably not, and neither did the politicians – but surely she should have known that two large pictures, complete with frames and glass would be so heavy, when you already carried the clothes of the family and had to hold in one hand, the small hand of a two and a half year old frightened child? Me. About to become a Catholic, Irish, immigrant child.

Back to that little two-roomed Irish home which also contained a wooden chest, the top of which could double for a hard bed in some emergency of hospitality. It had some books inside, remnants of great uncle Pat's studies at Trinity college, Dublin, before he went to America as a young man to be a teacher, only to return a few years later, disappointed and disillusioned, to marry great aunt Anne and, together, childless, they would bring up my mother, whose parents had emigrated to America, leaving her sadly, but understandably behind. (I will tell that story later). The chest and books then were reminders to Uncle Pat of failure, even trauma, and my mother was strictly forbidden to explore them. All her life she kept a yearning and reverence for learning. (She knew from a sly peek that Shakespeare had written "Othello – the Moor of Venice"!) It was a learning that for herself was totally forbidden. By Uncle Pat and his demons. As was travel to the big school in Westport where she was considered bright enough to go. It was this fact later, I am sure, that would explain her delight and pride at my being awarded a State Scholarship as a seventeen- year old, and with it my funds and chance to go to university. It was a prospect that all around the neighbourhood was condemned as foolishness when I was so obviously needed by the family, to go to work and help at home, since the nine younger children beneath me were still a heavy duty on my parents. My mother and father seemed oblivious to the tittle tattle and innuendo – I went to Manchester university with their full blessing. Perhaps to study Othello "Moor of Venice"! I remember now, with a tear in my eye, the day they both accompanied me to the railway station to say goodbye, and me in my brand new green winter coat and a perky matching beret on my head!

Back we go, though, to the days of my infancy! If there were few possessions indoors in that little Irish homestead, the dogs, on the outside, the cats, the hens, the pigs, the cow – even the big black bull on his occasional passion-fuelled visits, were familiar enough to be considered furniture and possessions to a little child. I had John, my dear mischievous asthmatic brother, of course, three years old, and Helen, my sister, older by two years, who hovered always between seniority and a vulnerability often denied.

We all had the love too of mother's Uncle Pat and Auntie Annie, so it could only have been a rich and lively life, often dominated by the seasons and the extreme changes in that Atlantic weather. These two foster parents of my mother, Pat and Annie, had welcomed her back home to Kiltimagh when after a failed first attempt to settle in England with her husband, she suffered a brutal forceps birth with her first born, John Patrick, in Coventry, supervised, she told me by a doctor reeking of drink. She had first joined my father in that city in 1934 after her marriage. Her health had been seriously jeopardised by the birth of John junior with internal wounds that took over a year to heal. Baby John, only months old, already had asthma and she had little choice but to return home to Ireland recover. My dad stayed in England to make some money and Pat and Annie helped to restore my dear mother to health and lovingly cared for the additional children born to her in Ireland. Those children being Helen and myself.

The cherishing I received myself perhaps can only be described by a little anecdote. I had a little ducky chair to rock in before I could walk and one day, one of the farm-dogs, wandering in front of me to gain the fire, received on his tail a firm yank from my baby fist. He bolted in fear, I held on tight, And up went ducky chair whilst baby was deposited flat on her nose on the big flagstone surrounds of the fire, that doubled as a dancing area when there was a celebration and the fiddlers were in.

The repercussions to this domestic disaster lasted for years. Never again would a dog be allowed in our house, in Ireland or England. (The embargo only collapsed thirty years later when my tenth sibling, fifteen-year old sister Margaret's inflexible will broke my mother's resistance, and the black mongrel Bengo arrived in our house in Tile Hill. But I was long gone then and married with four small children of my own – and only visited, as often as I could, travelling the five hour journey from Summerseat in Lancashire where we had come to form our own family).

Worse still, my mother tormented herself that I had irreparably flattened my nose and would be damaged for life. Hence, she subjected me at bedtime to sessions of "nose-pulling" to ensure my nose grew straight! How she grieved that she may have been responsible for a loss of beauty in her little girl! It became for me a ritual, second only to bedtime prayers and later the rosary. As an adult sometimes, as I studied her profile (usually as she held her head back to study a crossword puzzle) I saw that the graceful elegance of her own nose could never have been matched by mine – pulled or un-pulled! It always reminded me though of how deeply she cared and with what devotion she worried over her children – no less when there were twelve, than when there were three.

There were plenty of other dramas in that little

household. The boneens arriving in the night and the adults rushing to sit with them before the old sow had them devoured! The visit of the black bull that terrified Helen, even from inside the house, and the wonder of hearing the report that my mum had ridden him in her daring, carefree youth! (I know, from listening to conversations with fellow Irish immigrant friends that she had been reputed to be the fastest runner in Kiltimagh, "Until I caught her," my dad had slyly said!) The milking of the cows, the butter-making, the saving of the butter milk for the big loaves of soda bread baked in the ovens beside the turf fire. There was the potato harvest and the turf digging and stacking, this latter done in the bogs and probably the most important job on the farm because it was the turf fire that warmed the house in the cold Atlantic winters and cooked the food whatever the season, and never had to be rationed because the bogs themselves were so much more reliable than the fields in yielding their booty. There was too the weekly three-mile trip to market to sell surplus butter and eggs and buy flour and other household necessities – in the cart that had wheels nearly as high as the cottage ceiling. The other trip each week would be to attend mass in the stately imposing church in Kiltimagh, that towered on the main road, above all surrounding buildings. How did people so poor find the money to build such a church and how could mere peasants afford the elaborate gravestones in the adjacent graveyard, depicting life-size angels, Madonnas, statues of the Sacred

Heart and so many Pietas?

It was in later years I was told that it was in the choir balcony of that church, that Black and Tan soldiers from England (The scum of the British army, people said) had hidden, disguised in women's clothes, ready to leap out and denounce the priest at the most solemn moment of the mass. The reason being of course that he was accused of uttering some sentiment showing sympathy or worse for the I.R.A (Irish Republican Army). My parents always had a healthy disgust for the I.R.A, equalled only by their disgust for the Black and Tans and English soldiers, and their strategy was one of low profile and bemused indifference – but when the Church of God was profaned one could not be quiet.

"Didn't they know the ordinary people wanted none of either of them?" my mother would say. "And didn't the Irish make fools of themselves – they spent centuries fighting to be free of the English and then when they are free, they have to spoil it by fighting each other!" "But how can you ever forgive men who come like that into God's own house?" Shooting rifles across their school room whilst little children cowered under desks was never spoken of with the same contempt as the desecration that took place frequently during Sunday mass.

Cooking was a major part of daily life. A huge black cauldron hung over the fire for bacon and cabbage, a boiled chicken (perhaps at Christmas), pig's feet, or much more often, great potatoes in their skins to be eaten with a spot of butter or milk boiled with an onion. There were a hundred varieties of potatoes, my mother told me, "fit for a king". But her King was in England and one day there appeared in the cottage a little white envelope with money to buy the tickets for the long trip across Ireland by train to Dublin, and then to board the boat across the rough Irish sea, followed by the train down from Holyhead to the busy and fast growing, industrial city of Coventry in the County of Warwickshire, as it was then named, before some bureaucrat labelled it West Midlands. Changing history into geography!

*

Momentous tickets indeed – to go to England and to face, like most immigrants – all the changes and dangers and uncertainties that lay ahead. At the age of two and a half, the little Catholic, Irish child was to become a Catholic, Irish, immigrant child. She was to meet John, the man she hardly knew, her dark-haired father, and was to leave the country of Eire behind. The country, the breeze and terrifying lightning storms from the Atlantic, and that very special county – "The County of Mayo!"

2

Journey and Arrival
"If You Ever Go Across the Sea to England....."

It was 1940. The Second World War, provoked by Germany's invasion of Poland, had lasted nearly a year and many of Coventry's prestigious car factories had been requisitioned to make munitions for the war effort and needed more and more workers. The Rileys, the Daimlers, the Fords, the Rolls Royces, the Hillmans, the Standards, the Triumphs, the Jaguars – the whole world-wide famous car industry was to be put into mothballs so that these highly skilled workers could produce the vehicles, aircraft, and the munitions needed so desperately for the war effort.

At last it had seemed, to that young Irish, immigrant man of twenty-six, John, Thomas O' Brien, that all the labouring, badly-paid work on the buildings could become a thing of the past. (Coventry Technical college still stands proudly today in the Butts and this was one of my dad's first employments when he came to England as a boy of nineteen, with only five pound in his pocket, as uncle Martin, his youngest brother told me at his funeral). No, it seemed certain now that there would be enough regular work for my father to secure a living for his wife, three children and one more still in the womb. There would be as much overtime as you wanted in those frantic munition's factories and for my parents there was little choice. With such a swiftly growing family, life could no longer be sustained on the little, infertile farm of 28 acres in Kiltimagh. Auntie Annie and Uncle Pat had more than fulfilled their duty of care to my mother since in 1915 her own mother had left her, taking her brother John, to join her husband, Michael Mullaney, in Philadelphia, Pennsylvania, U.S.A, where he worked as a ship's stoker.

*

This is the sad story of that occurrence. It is the explanation of how my mother came to be left, bereft, in Kiltimagh where Aunt Annie and Uncle Pat were to bring her up as their own.

Tickets had been bought for my grandmother Delia, (or Bridget as she was more commonly known) to sail to America to join her husband, Michael in Philadelphia. It was there that they had first met and married, but like my mother returning to England in 1934, Grandmother Bridget had returned to Ireland for a few years while her husband found a suitable house for them. There were three children then (and I couldn't help reflecting how history repeats itself with mam taking us three to England!) Things were to go tragically awry! Before the sailing date my mother, Annie, then aged three, Tommy aged five and her big brother John, aged seven, contracted what was then, before antibiotics, the deadly scarlet fever. Little Tommy died. Grandmother Bridget, distraught, wanted nothing but to get to her husband Michael in the States where he had a home for them, even if in the most run down area of Philadelphia.

Young John at seven, recovered well. My mother though, aged only three, lingered in the illness and when the sailing date came only grandmother and young John were deemed fit to sail and pass the rigorous tests that would be imposed at Ellis island, the immigration entrance for the United States. By fluke of fate or maybe just the workings of the human heart, Auntie Annie and Uncle Pat, devastated already to be losing the whole family, couldn't have been happier to keep care of my mum (Didn't I tell you already that when grandmother Bridget first stayed in Ireland while husband Michael found a home for her and the three children in Philadelphia, that it had been Uncle Pat and Aunt Annie who had given them all a home?). Grandmother, though, with a heart hardened by the death of her little child swore she never again would set foot in the land that had stolen her son Tommy. In other words, she would nevermore return to her daughter Annie or to Kiltimagh. My mother then would never see her father and the rest of her family in America. My dear mother then was to remain in Kiltimagh with her aunt and uncle and was soon to be replaced in Grandmother Bridget's affections by the later Mullaney children born in America, Mary, Michael Junior, Martin and Alice.

It was half a century later that mum was to learn the full truth of all this. Secrets and lies. Her own father, never to see his little daughter with the lovely, curly, auburn hair that needed seven plaits to tame it for school, several times sent money for daughter Annie to be brought to America. It was never revealed to her. Her mother refused to countenance her existence or else convinced herself that Annie was better off where she was. There was even a suggestion that she may have intercepted the money but Aunt Annie and Uncle Pat continued to love her dearly and, perhaps afraid to lose her, asked and answered no questions, and my mother grew with the pain of rejection and loss deeply hidden in her heart.

She told me many times how she was taken to the station to say goodbye to her mother and brother, John, and had screamed in terror at the sound of the train as it left the station. She was never to see her mother again, and her brother, John, only fifty years later. Of her father she had only a few precious letters he had written to her. She always claimed, that until the day she died, she could hear. as clear as a bell, the noise of that train in her ears. And how it made her want to scream.

Now, at the tender age of twenty-seven my mother was reliving her own mother's experience of leaving her native land by train. By God's grace though, she had her three children with her and one of her first unlikely actions on arriving in England was to have a photographer film those three little urchins, with their high buttoned boots and rather scruffy coats! Their eyes were bright though and

interested and they knew they were with one that loved them dearly. For my mother though, life was intimidating and even at many times hostile. She said she was mortally terrified of the gas stove in case it should explode. She had only ever cooked and baked with a turf fire. She was perplexed by the strange little gas mantles that hung from the ceiling and lit with a pop and shrouded the room in yellow. Although more dangerous, she preferred the candles that stood in a saucer and lit the bedrooms where there was no gas. She was also in a foreign land. At that time the Irish were not entirely welcome, factory fodder or not. A common notice on the doors of lodging houses or cheap hotels was "No Blacks, No children, No Irish", or in restaurants where it read "No Blacks, No Irish, No Dogs".

But we weren't just from Ireland, we were from Kiltimagh, Mayo, Ireland! It wasn't for nothing that the common response to a confession of coming from Mayo was the exclamation, "Mayo, God help us!" Spoken with a mixture of sympathy and more than a hint of contempt! Nor was it a coincidence that the further revelation of coming from Kiltimagh drew the even more damning, "So you're a Kiltchie then?" – and this was much more painful ridicule! After all one born in the poorest town of the poorest county in the furthermost tip of Western Ireland, could only be a complete idiot!

Those critics, fellow Irishmen from middle and eastern Ireland, as well as English strangers, didn't stop to think that within a few miles from Kiltimagh rose the most holy mountain in Ireland, Croagh Patrick, esteemed for nearly fifteen hundred years, and where Saint Patrick himself had gone to fast for forty days in emulation of his Saviour Jesus Christ, who had himself fasted in the desert for forty days before the beginning of his ministry. Nor did they remember that it was that same Saint Patrick that was he who inaugurated the Celtic Christianity and was rumoured to have settled first in County Mayo when he returned again to Ireland and began the mission that was to convert huge swathes of Europe to Christianity, including Northern England and Scotland. They didn't know that now, even in the twenty first century, over a million people a year climb the reek (Croagh Patrick), each year in pilgrimage as witness to their profound faith in Christianity. And they still climb that mountain, but not so often as my parents in their youth had, in their bare feet to attest their faith and strengthen it.

Nor did those same mockers stop to think that only a few miles away in the small town of Knock in 1879, ravaged still by continuing bouts of potato blight persisting intermittently since the great famine of 1846 and struggling against poverty and starvation, there had been an apparition of the Blessed Virgin Mary, St. John the Evangelist and Saint Joseph, on the southern gable of the parish church in Knock. Beside them and a little to the right was an altar with a cross and the figure of a lamb, around which angels hovered. There were fifteen official witnesses who stood and watched this vision for two hours in the pouring rain. Knock was approved by the rigorous examinations of the Catholic church in two commissions of enquiry in 1879 and 1936 and today is a major Marian shrine. Pope John Paul II was to visit in the centenary year of 1979, and a thriving airport strangely, against the commercial common sense of every business man in the land, has been successfully established in what was considered for so long, the most God-forsaken place in Eire! I digress more, sorry:

As a child I had remembered that Jesus Himself had been mocked for His origins, "Can anything good come from Nazareth?" Nathanial had asked sceptically, and maybe it was that reminder that kept in my heart a sort of fierce pride beneath the fears, shame and insecurities of being an Irish, Catholic immigrant child from the little town of Kiltimagh.

*

Back to my mother though, as she survived her journey and joined her husband in his bachelor lodgings in Coventry. "Thin as a bone he was," she told us later, "and a hole in his shin with a festering wound." But despite her despair, the wound healed very fast with our arrival. But I never did understand why she should be shocked at his thinness though, because until the day he died he never seemed to gain a pound. He ate well but seldom, he smoked his few woodbines, confessing to us that he'd taken his first puffs at eight, and he worked indefatigably, in the factory and at home. "He never had a pick on him," people used to say. Five foot, ten inches tall, with legs that seemed more than half his length. We used to laugh at the long strides he took when we had to run to keep up. His hair was black, thick and straight, and fell to the side with a long, shiny swoop. Many a man would have been proud of such hair – with hardly a grey hair when he died – but he never left the house without it hidden under his flat cap. (I tell a lie. Recently I saw a video from the early days of Our Lady of the Assumption church, where we went when I was fifteen, and father in the Eucharistic processions was of course bare headed, and so handsome still, in his mid-forties.)

Even in his hospital bed, in his pyjamas, and a short distance from his death, he put on the flat cap in defiance of the nurses. "I want to go home," he said to his youngest granddaughter, "Come on Maria, let's go home." Like many an Irish man his cap was part of his identity, as was the tin whistle he kept always in his inside pocket. He was like the Pied Piper whose fingers were ever straying, his music to be playing. God bless the man! But what of the three little urchins? "You cried on the train," my mother said, "you cried on the boat. You cried on the train again, and worst of all, your poor father, when you saw him, you cried, even more!"

 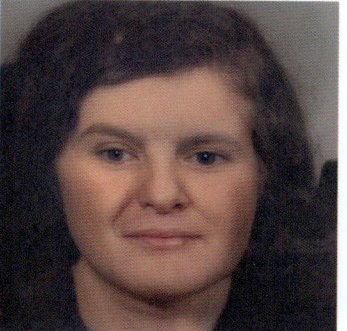

I wondered afterwards if that was when his habit started of always telling us poems and stories at bedtime before our prayers, became a way of winning the love of his little ones. Or each Sunday, taking us to mass with him and benediction, to kneel on the very front row, smell the wonderful incense and see all that was happening on the altar. Or perhaps it was his habit of always playing the tin whistle in the evening when my mother cooked the meal (He told me that he could play the flute well, even before his first fag, at seven, and earned precious money for his family by going with the carol singers at Christmas to play his accompaniment). Whatever the strategies, he won us over completely, and as if in honour of my new-found love, he re-Christened me. Now I was to be called Christine, my second name, or Chrissie, and little Annie was forgotten - I was now truly a Catholic, Irish, immigrant child.

3

The Blitz

"From the Bogs to the Bombs"

Moving from the cramped lodgings of a working man, my parents found for us a little terraced house in Henry street in the middle of Coventry. It was 1940, remember. My brother Michael, often called Mick, or Micky, was inexplicably born, (for me that is) at the end of June, amidst the increasing alarms of sirens and raids and houses on fire. There was gas mask distribution, ration books, black-out instructions and concrete cubic shelters appearing in the middle of streets. Of the new home in Henry Street I have no memory, and that doesn't matter much because one night in October when we were all in the shelter, it was bombed to the ground. From June of that year, after a time when people had relaxed thinking perhaps that the war wouldn't be so bad and most of the children evacuated in the first pronouncement of war had returned to their parents, air-raids had started for the first time over Coventry – small sporadic affairs and sufficient only to cause the sirens to go and sensible people to break their sleep, grab their gas masks and head to the municipal air-raid shelter.

According to my mother this was an almost nightly occurrence and so very tiring. How did she cope taking tiny baby Michael out with his bottle of milk going cold? Although we three older children had been breast fed to the age of nine months as was the custom in Ireland, I'm not at all surprised that amidst the stress and commotion of the night-time bombings, my mother couldn't succeed with Mick. Fortunately, it was summertime so we didn't suffer too badly from the cold.

In October, however things changed for Coventry. For on the 8th and the 14th of that month the raids became vicious. Apparently from 1936 the Coventry factories had started to be prepared for a transition to war production. The Whitley, Lancaster and Stirling engines were all produced in Coventry for the English bombing planes. The Daimler, Rootes and the Standard factories were commissioned to make Hercules engines. The Alvis and Rolls Royce works made the Merlin engines for the famous Spitfire planes and the Daimler concentrated on armoured cars, Alfred Herbert manufactured machine tools and other military equipment, whilst the Standard eventually produced the Mosquito. These facts I found out much later and I also learned that the Luftwaffe had detailed very accurate plans of all the ex-car plants which were now, in 1940, building planes and munitions as well as armoured vehicles. Hitler realised that raids on London and other cities were not sufficient and Coventry in particular must become a key target if he was to win the war. There was also the suggestion made that by making this raid on Coventry frighteningly intensive according to area, people throughout the land would be cowed into submission.

*

So it happened. The very same night that our house in Henry street was razed to the ground, on October 12th, the air-raid shelter we had sought refuge in, was also hit. If we had been in the house, we would all have been killed, but were so "lucky" to be in the shelter. For there, out of twenty-seven occupants only ten were killed. I read later that it had been a big surface shelter about 15 to 20 feet square, with a cap of 10-12ins thick reinforced concrete. The blast of the bomb from a few feet away had demolished the supporting walls and the whole roof had come down on all of us people inside. So, ten dead was a pretty good outcome considering.

My brother John was hit by a piece of falling masonry which badly fractured his skull. And dear sister Helen, on the ground was trampled on by a hob-nailed boot, worn by some man in the terror of his life, trying to escape. At the hospital later they said that the indentations of the sole of the boot could be clearly seen on her poor, torn mouth. "What blackguard," I can hear my father saying, "would stand on the face of a tiny little child, to escape the chance of the roof collapsing on him?" Daddy would have overlooked the fact that the roof had already collapsed nor would he have realised perhaps that people having undergone one huge trauma, inevitably are tuned to expect a second. But maybe, I reflect on it myself, that that man, like so many others on that night, was concussed and didn't know what he was doing.

A gentleman called Albert Hearn took my mother's arm and helped her climb over the rubble with baby Mick in her arms. Albert, himself in memoirs, remembered the event as his rescue of a woman with a child of fifteen months. Michael was not even three months then but knowing my mum and her terror of a child catching cold, she probably had him wrapped in ten thick blankets and anyone looking would expect to see a giant inside! Perhaps it was all the padding that saved him from worse injury? Who knows? Or the grace of God?

This same man, Albert Hearn – "God bless the mark" as my mother would say! – was later to receive the George medal, that highest award possible for civilian bravery, for working tirelessly with a rescue squad during this night of October 12th and saving innumerable lives, some of them from the Henry Street shelter. I later read that he had tunnelled under debris to pull out several people, even though at that time there was a gas alert from a broken gas pipe.

*

But, where was I? There was no sign of me. I seemed to have

vanished. There was no time to lose with looking. My mother, with three-month baby Michael was helped over the rubble before more of the roof fell in. My dad and his friend Mr. Duffy carried John and Helen in their blood and pain and went as directed to a pub nearby. (They called it a rescue centre.) My mother, beside herself, confronted the air-raid wardens and begged them to take Helen and John to the nearby Coventry and Warwickshire hospital. They refused. The orders were, they said, that it was too dangerous to venture outside with the number of bombs falling.

But, where was I?

Something must have happened to me. Someone must return to the shelter, my dad decided, and Mr. Duffy, (a fellow immigrant from Mayo) must come too. My mother was to be left in the pub, with John and Helen and three-month old Michael. When the two men arrived at the ruins of the shelter no child was there. A few people were scrabbling in the rubble, perhaps for some precious item lost in the blast. Perhaps too they had lost a child? Perhaps I had been buried too? Someone, hearing of their predicament, gave my dad a shovel. It was a tool he had had plenty of experience with, and would for the rest of his life, (God bless the man) He never told me later what he had felt then, as he dug, while the gallant Mr Duffy scrabbled with his bare hands. A little bit of a coat emerged. A small face coated with dust and cement. A little foot missing a shoe. No crying as he scooped me up, unharmed without a scratch, but with dirt and plaster in my mouth and lungs. He held me to his chest, and I was safe.

The two men returned once more to the pub bearing their trophy – but there were two other children now in much more need than this little dusty Lazarus, who hadn't even the grace to cry! I can imagine clinging to my mam as my dad and Mr. Duffy took matters into their own hands and with the adamant refusal of the Home guard to accompany them and against every warning, they ventured out into the maelstrom of fire and explosions of that terrible blitz, to carry John and Helen to the hospital. Lucky, they did. John's fracture was serious, and he was to spend four months in a hospital outside the city and return a frightened little boy who briefly suffered nightmares.

In the Coventry and Warwickshire hospital they said Helen's wounded mouth was so serious it would never heal without an operation. But the very night before the appointed day of operation, when visited by the emergency surgeon, Helen's mouth had shown a near miraculous change and improvement, with a lot of the sepsis gone. The doctor said if he was religious, he would have called it a miracle. She would no longer need an operation. But she would be transferred outside the city to recover in safety. She was there for over a month, just long enough to survive the worst blitz of all, the one when over 500 in the city were killed and over half of the city destroyed in a barrage that lasted from 7pm to the all clear at 11am the following day.

*

This was to be the great November Blitz recently commemorated for its anniversary of seventy-five years throughout the city of Coventry. It was the blitz when 1,000 high explosives were dropped and over 30,000 incendiary bombs. 75 factories were destroyed and half the city's housing stock. The beautiful mediaeval Cathedral of Saint Michael's in central Broadgate took a direct hit and amazingly the spire was left standing intact. Not too far away our very own beloved church of Saint Osburg's standing at the top of Hill Street also took a hit but was left, like the Cathedral with spire intact. The school adjacent also was bombed by aircraft intent on hitting the gasometer nearby. The damage to the city was such as to coin a new word for calamitous damage in warfare. It was the term to "Coventrate." Hitler had certainly made his point. It was said that throughout the war no other city sustained, according to its size, the intensity of obliteration suffered as that of Coventry during that sixteen-hour onslaught on November 14th, 1940.

4

Another Household
"Life in a Court – Dickensian Style!"

God knows how my parents found another little house to live in after Henry Street was bombed. Half of Coventry must have been looking for a new place. You would think there'd be empty houses galore as people fled the city with the nightly bombardments that continued throughout October and early November, culminating in the devastation of the great blitz, but strangely that didn't happen. Since so many had been destroyed, houses became indeed hard to find and a little two-roomed hovel became our home for the next year or so. With a speed that was breath-taking, all the major services were restored to the city. Like the Phoenix the city seemed to rise from the ashes.

Our new home was in the centre of the city, near the Butts, and it was in a court, in Thomas Street. It was the sort of place you would associate with a London slum in Dickensian times. It was a dark, scary place and I know this because I visited the place again as a small child to play with children there. From the street you went down a narrow alley-way to where twelve or more tiny two-roomed houses flanked a square courtyard at whose centre stood a small water tap that was the source of water for all the families that had settled there. The one room downstairs was a sort of living-room-kitchen warmed by a big black-lead coal fireplace and the coal for this fire was stored in a big cupboard, called the coal-house, behind the table where we ate, usually standing, because I can only recall two upright chairs in the room. It's hard to imagine how the room was furnished. There was the big black-lead fire place, fed with the coal from the coal-house, some sort of sink without taps because the water came from the tap outside, a small gas cooking stove and some place where my parents slept with baby Michael. What was it? A couch? A fold-up mattress? Whatever it was it couldn't have taken up much room in that diminutive cottage. My parents told us later that one heavy raid was so sudden there wasn't a hope of getting to the shelter and so we all had to cram into the coal house for safety.

"How could we?" I later asked myself. It was only about five feet high inside and about three feet across, with a ceiling that sloped under the stairs, from about six to three feet in height. How could we all fit in there? And sit on top of filthy lumps of coal? My mum and dad and John and Helen and me and baby Michael – how on earth could we? But we did, and it spared us from being hit by a bomb as we ran to the nearest shelter.

Two or three brick-built toilets stood in a separate block in the left hand corner of the court, fronted by huge mounds of ashes and refuse, where people dumped the remains of their fires and the stuff that couldn't be burnt in them. Perhaps there were a few dustbins nearby but they were probably overflowing and never emptied. I have no memory of ever doing "wee, wee" or "po" in those dark and smelly chambers and I feel sure that my mother would have let me use a chamber pot and would have emptied it there herself. For some of the time she had only me and baby Michael to care for while Helen and John were in hospital. But surely enough, with my dad always working overtime and so many nights broken by trips to the shelter after the siren had sounded, Hitler hadn't slowed the war effort completely. Within months the men had all the work they wanted as the munition and vehicle production resumed.

After a few months, Helen and John were returned to us, John with brief but terrifying night terrors that meant he slept downstairs with mum and dad. He recovered fast to be as much a live wire as ever. With Helen though, her fears were to persist for a lifetime. She screamed always to hear the coming of a plane. She was terrified of thunder and lightning and even when an adult was known to squeeze into the space under the stairs with the coming of a storm. She woke at the smallest noise, a torture to me years later, when we shared a bed and she woke with my page-turning as I tried desperately to read by the light of a torch and she would hear the rustle and "tell on me". Many of these terrors persisted sadly into her adult life. Hardly surprising.

At six years of age she was much more aware than me and the trauma of her mouth injury and the experience of intense pain, was followed so abruptly by separation from those she loved. I myself had sleep-walked through my burial experience and instead of separation, I had received extra attention and love. That would explain one of my earliest memories of those post-blitz days. My mother took me to visit our nearest church, Saint Osburg's, the oldest Catholic church in Coventry. In that Great Blitz, that brought King George himself to our city, Hitler, aiming at the big gasometer on Hill Street, had missed his target and as I already said, hit Saint Osburg's church and the adjacent school. It was the school that John and Helen had already attended and whose wonders had been boasted about to me as an Aladdin's Cave of treasures that lay in waiting for me when I too was five and could go to school. Although only four, I can recall the bitterest of disappointments to learn I could no longer look forward to that paradise. The church too, like the lovely Cathedral of Saint Michael's in the middle of Coventry, now a healing monument to mankind's desire for Reconciliation, had taken a direct hit. In both cases the central nave of the church and roof were destroyed, but miraculously, the spires were left standing.

What was it that drove my mother that day, to leave baby Michael to be looked after by someone else, to take me to her beloved church, to clamber over masonry and broken glass and to find a place to kneel in prayer? I remember how high the rubble was and, as a small child of three, how hard it was to step through all the debris. And how, when you looked up, you saw the sky. Did my mother come in thanksgiving that my life had been spared that month before, when I was buried in the bombing of the shelter at Henry street? Or was she praying that John and Helen would survive their injuries? Or perhaps in fact was she offering a thanksgiving for the life of each one of us, including the new life she must have known by then, she was carrying? This was Thomas, to be born at the end of June a year to the day after the birth of baby Michael. Or was it maybe to pray most earnestly for her two little children. John and Helen, grievously injured in hospital? Or perhaps she had the strongest need to place herself in the hands of God, in order to cope with all the trials and difficulties that she knew lay ahead. All I knew was that I was proudly with her in that ruined church and drank in her awe and hope. I looked forward very much too to going with her to the second-hand clothes shop at the bottom of Hill Street. I loved "new clothes" even then.

5

Evacuation

"Cut to the Quick – and Not Just the Nails."

Thomas Street may have been ugly, cramped, and frightening but it was home because we were with each other. The nightly sorties to the several different shelters, bundled in thick clothes against the cold, were routine. Helen fell over the water tap in the middle of the court, in the dark of the blackout and she screamed and screamed. But we just had to accept a certain amount of screaming then.

    Standards were kept though and when mother noticed that some jam was missing from the precious jam pot, she knew immediately that John had pinched a spoonful on our return from the shelter. (He told us later, he was always so hungry after an air-raid and would eat even toothpaste if he could get it!). He was hit, for a punishment, hand or stick, I'm not sure – but it was indeed a very serious matter, that made me cry. In our house, even as we grew to young adulthood there was never a finger laid on a girl, but it was customary for the boys to receive a clout, usually of the hand, though I do remember once my dad taking his belt off to John. (I have a feeling it was an act of bravado that meant he wouldn't stand for bad behaviour.) It was probably good that he did because I remember later during the war years how many of the local boys disappeared off to "approved school" or similar detention centres. With fathers away at war and mothers sometimes distracted by the attentions of American soldiers it wasn't too surprising that children should get into trouble. I'm not sure you could judge the severity of any paternal punishment by the din of the roaring that ensued in the case of John! (Most of it was theatrical and my mum later teased him with the story of how he had retreated to his bed to "roar" for some punishment given, and mother, being curious, peeked round the corner to see if he was alright, found him carefully studying his own face in a mirror to see how sad he was!)

My strongest memory of this time in Thomas Street was a certain contentment. I don't remember fear. I felt maybe distaste and disgust. It was by any standard ugly. It was squalid. It was cramped and claustrophobic, but we were together. Perhaps I let Helen take all the fear and John take all the hunger. I felt adored. I felt greatly secure in the love of my parents. (My poor dad, he told us later, had been rejected to serve in the armed forces because of the particularly painful and chronic acne that he suffered on his back. It would have made it impossible for him to carry the heavy kit bags of a soldier.) I do remember though how his pride was hurt that he should be considered less of a man than many of the "Lachecos" he had seen enlisted. For me it meant my dear daddy was still with us to take us to mass on Sunday morning and often to Benediction on Sunday afternoon where I loved the smell of incense. He was there too to kneel with us to say the rosary, the words of which we knew long before the age of five. And then of course his bedtime offering of a recitation of some famous ballad learned by heart in his own school days. Oh, "The Wreck of the Hesperus" and "Lord Ullin's Daughter" how we loved them!

I felt secure. My mother told me about the occasion when she had introduced me to Mrs Keens (who owned the little shop at the top of Thomas Street where we bought the daily bread). I had said to her as way of introduction, "I'm Christine. Do you like me? I'm only three and a half." My mother fondly reminded me of this as evidence of my endearing ways. Surely a child would only ask such a question if convinced the answer would be in the affirmative! And unless they had some sense of their own precocity! And so it was, for Mrs Keens always did like me, and I her, and for many, many years we kept a fond and faithful relationship as I became the chief bread-fetcher for the family, on my return from school and this lasted until I was fifteen, still attending Grammar school, and we moved to Tile Hill. When I heard of her death I cried. I must have been nearly eighteen then and hadn't seen her for three years.

"Three loaves please and a penny worth of mint imperials!" was my daily request when I went to her shop after school, and what was an amazing thing – I was not even asked by Mrs Keens for the ration coupons for sweets, even though each child's entitlement was only four ounces a week. This "three loaf order" was probably a later daily bread order when my family had grown, along with the appetites. I liked Mrs Keens most dearly and she was just one of the loved ones I missed when I was evacuated. The other dear heart of mine at this time was my baby brother Michael. I thought he was mine because that was his name – "My Chael." How I cried those words again and again when my mother, at six months pregnant was obliged to go to a convent in Leamington to have baby Tommy and escape the dangers of the bombing and we four children had to be evacuated. I was separated from "My Chael". My dad was left at home alone to continue his long days' work at Dunlop's, the rubber and tyre factory, as part of the war effort.

What must my mother have felt to have left her four children, two not long recovered from their shelter wounds and one a little "shiner" (so they said, all peace and smiles and clever little ways?) But most of all to leave baby Michael, at nine months of age now, already so hard to take the bottle. (Put off no doubt by all the cold milk he had had to drink in the long hours of the night as we sought safety in the shelter, (before the days of vacuum flasks to keep a baby's milk warm.)

*

They say you don't remember very much before you are three or four years of age, but I disagree. I think if something affects you profoundly when you are small, it can stay with you all your life. That was how it was with me with the evacuation experience and the particular way it was done. It's hard to know how the authorities made their decisions then (and maybe now). But certainly, child psychology didn't come into it. Helen and John, being over five were to go to a place called Town Thorns, which I believe had been an open-air school outside Birmingham, for children with asthma. At least those two were kept together, though Helen told me later that she blacked it all out so totally that she couldn't even remember John being there at all. Since I was between the ages of two and five, I had to go to a little converted nursery school in somewhere called the "Licky Hills", near the Malvern hills. It was also on the other side of Birmingham.

*

The next time I heard of this place was when Pope Benedict in 2013 came to nearby Croxley park, during a papal visit to England and Scotland to officiate at the mass that beatified the famous and holy Cardinal, John Henry Newman. I had the chance to experience just how far away from Coventry was Licky Hills when, as a parish group, with our Vietnamese priest Fr Michael Ho Huu Nghia, we went to see the Pope and participate in that beatification mass. We travelled by coach and as I relaxed physically on that comfortable journey, my mind and heart travelled the same journey on a rusty old bike as my dad had travelled in 1941 when he came to visit me. I told my friend Terry Allen about it, confessing my sadness. She wisely reminded me: "How he must have loved you!"

It was the only time I was to see one of the family in three months. I was alone of the family at the Licky Hill's home and not even four years of age. I remember so much of it vividly, as though pictures were carved for all time on my brain. I remember the shaky little camp beds we slept on, close to the floor. Because we were so little it was probably a safety measure in case we fell out of bed – and there were no cots to use. I remember looking at a bathroom door and high up there were lists of writing. I knew when the nurses studied it that it told them who was to have a special bath that day. I know that it hurt a lot to be scrubbed and when our fingernails were cut, it was right down to the quick, so you sucked your fingers in pain afterwards. My mother never cut my nails like that. The memory most vivid though was to take place on a roasting hot Sunday in June. My mother later told me that it was on this day that my father cycled the long distance from Coventry to visit me. "Your poor dad," she said. "I don't even know where he got the old wreck of a bike. You rarely saw a bike in those days. It must have been nearly thirty miles for him to ride and he was collapsing with the heat. But he saw you! And he told me."

My memory starts after he left. After the visitors had gone the nurses took out a selection of wheeled toys for all of us little ones to play with. They were distributed. I was given a doll's pram. A boy near me was given a little bike. I wanted the bike.

Did I want to be like my dad? Did I want to follow my dad on that little bike and go home with him? Either way, there must have been a very powerful motivation because, although usually a gentle, sweet-tempered child, I hit the boy and dragged the bike from him. A huge and horrible nurse descended on me. She pulled me screaming to a nearby glass house and locked me in. I could only stand there and look out through the glass, and the memory of her terrifying face glaring down on me, imprinted itself forever on my mind.

How indelible was this image? Well, as a student at Manchester University, returning to my Hall of Residence, Saint Gabriel's, one late evening with a friend, we passed the glass kiosk of an all-night petrol garage. As I glanced up, I saw the same terrifying face I'd seen at Licky hills, staring down at me with hatred through the glass (there was a woman attendant sitting there.) I sank to my knees in fear and weakness. My friend was confused and worried but glad when I recovered enough to get to my feet and resume the journey home. I think it was later that night that I came to an understanding of what had frightened me so terribly. The attendant had probably glanced at us quite normally, but that hateful face from my evacuation was somehow triggered in my mind by a distant female image through glass.

*

But I haven't yet recounted what had happened to baby Michael in the days of the evacuation. Under twos were usually sent to a family rather than to an institution to be cared for. And Michael was only nine months then. Already a poor eater, my mother told me he refused food and drink completely and after a few weeks the authorities decided to move him from the first couple who had him, for fear he would die. "God is good", my mother said later, for the next family to have him, fell in love with him entirely and he began at last to take some nourishment and thrive. The family were called the Blundells. They lived outside of Birmingham, were well-to-do businesspeople and Quakers I believe, and my mother never forgot their goodness. When three months later, the time came for mum to bring the new little copper-headed baby home from his birthplace in the convent, in Leamington, (Thomas Joseph by name), the Blundells pleaded to be allowed to keep little Michael, they loved him so dearly. My mother, although intensely grateful, knew too much about the sadness of childhood separation to allow him to stay with them. Instead this kind, wealthy Quaker family became for a few years, guardian angels to the family, visiting often and bringing to us, all the way to Coventry, some of those necessities of life, lost in the blitz, like bedding and kitchen ware.

6

Vincent Street

"New Home, New Hope, Old Terrors"

When it came time for me to return home from my evacuation at Licky Hills, the family had moved once again. This time from the hateful and dark courtyard in Thomas Street to the comparative luxury of a four-roomed, terraced house in nearby Vincent Street. Vincent Street still exists today but it is in a different location, the old terraces being demolished in the post-war frenzy that saw much of the Elizabethan cottages of mediaeval Spon street needlessly razed to the ground as if they were as worthless as the many concrete shelters that after the war, still besmirched the centres of many streets in that area of the Butts.

Our house actually had its own running water, with a tap and sink indoors and although the toilet was still outdoors it was our very own. It stood a short distance from the house for the family's exclusive convenience. In our garden! Yes we actually had our own private, outdoor, tiny plot of land in England to replace the twenty-eight acres that in Ireland had been our spacious kingdom! The door of the toilet was on a latch though, so you were never totally sure of privacy! Little squares of newspaper were neatly tied in a pad at the side of the lavatory for use as toilet paper. (I'm sure however that it was never "News of the

World" because that paper was assigned to the Index as far as my family were concerned! I even recall a ban being placed on Helen and me visiting the house of a little friend because one of us had innocently referred to a reported story we had read there, of a vicar doing naughty things!) But back on topic, it was to be many, many years, long after the war was over, that toilet tissue paper became the norm.

Vincent Street was a short street of terraced houses, a cul-de-sac off Hope Street, that led to the Butts to the left and to the right, Trafalgar Street and Windsor Street; hence to Spon Street and up Barras Lane to Saint Osburg's Church and our school. I narrate here the route we children took every day of the week for five years at least, until that is, I, all alone, at the age of ten and three-quarters was to make my solitary progression from the turning to Saint Osburg's, up the long walk of Middleborough Road to Barr's Hill Grammar School. The left side of Windsor Street was total devastation with as many as twenty houses reduced to rubble and Spon Street was like a mouth with missing teeth, some pretty little cottages four hundred years old at least. left standing, others reduced to a gaping hole. Vincent Street however, had been left relatively intact. At its entrance from Hope Street on the left-hand side, were two huge, mysterious, locked warehouses. Was it a black-market depot I later wondered, because we children were never to see it opened in the daytime? From these there continued the residential houses numbering from two to twenty-four. This was our side of the street. Our house was number twenty. Houses twenty-six and twenty-eight had been obliterated by a bomb (or several) so the living accommodations ended in a vast, open, bombed site. The houses were to rent of course at ten shillings a week and during the ten years we lived there it never altered a penny. The funny little man in a raincoat made his appearance every Friday morning and duly signed the tatty little rent book when my mother paid him.

Although the worst of the debris had been cleared from the bombed houses, numbers 26 and 28, the site remained as a powerful reminder of Hitler's omnipresent danger. I remember as a tot, playing in the debris, constantly finding huge screeds of coils of metal shavings blown there from a bomb blast that had hit a factory across the River Sherbourne that flowed along the bottom of our gardens. Sometimes the metal even felt hot-perhaps from a raid the previous night. It was a constant reminder of Hitler and destruction, but also spoke loudly of the skill and accuracy of the German aerial bombardment that it could pinpoint so exactly the small munition factories that nestled along the bank of the river there. Some may have employed no more than ten or twenty men!

This bombed site however soon lost these doleful connections. In our childish private parlance, we referred to it as "Up the Top." And it became the centre of our life and play; of our friendships and social life; of our physical training and our ball skill development – even of our opportunities for hero-worship and admiring adulation as we encountered kids from many streets around who congregated there to play! In honour of "Up the Top" I will devote a whole chapter of my story to this significant, precious, unlikely, but indispensable location!

Raids continued sporadically once we were in our new home, the main difference being that we now had a wider choice of shelters and those that we trusted were much further away. The ones down Vincent Street were repugnant because of the suffocating smell of urine, dog or human, I'm not sure. Sometimes a wobbly tramp was seen to emerge unsteadily in the morning. One reliable set of shelters though was beneath the Butt's Technical college, yes, the same one my dad helped to build. Even now I proudly tell my many grandchildren when they come to visit me in Coventry, "Look at that fine building! Your great grandfather helped to build it when he was only nineteen years old!"

There was one memorable occasion when shelters alone were considered insufficient and orders came from the Home Guard that the occupants of all the streets around the Butts, should make their way up to the grassy acres of Hearsall Common to remain there in the open air for most the night. A more brutal assault than usual was expected. Although a tent was set up at the far end to offer tea, there were too many people for us to benefit from it. And it was very cold. We milled around, like sheep without a shepherd and at dawn were requested to leave as there had been a false alarm this time.

Another difference was the change in the sound of the bombs. Now you heard, as you stumbled to a shelter, a fearful, sharp whistling sound followed by an eerie silence. You knew the bomb was still coming, but where was it? I remembered at my tender age the sense of total disorientation. People panicked and screamed and began to run pell-mell dragging hysterical children. It seemed almost more desirable for a bomb to fall on your head than endure this abject terror.

The concrete shelters in the middle of the street left just enough room for the odd tradesman with his horse and cart, bringing milk or collecting rags. A big event was the arrival of the coal lorry. My mother gave a sigh of relief that for a little longer she could warm the house, boil the kettle or stew pot, and dry the endless supply of napkins needed, with two babies in the house as well as the clothes of us three dirty children. I try now to envision the day of the coal delivery when half hundred weight sacks were carried on the backs of black, begrimed coal-men, who tramped on filthy feet to dump the coal in the coal house at the back of the kitchen, in the space under the stairs. Outside the boys gathered to hang on the back of the lorry and get a free ride. Whether any of the coal was filched I can't say for certain, but for sure there was plentiful droppings that people scurried for – just as eagerly as they scurried to shovel into buckets the steaming manure left by the horses which were still used for delivery services when petrol was almost inaccessible.

And to this new home I returned from the evacuation at Licky hills in a little pink woolly coat and with an unusual layer of plumpness! I remember standing, strangely bashful, beside my mother, next to the main street lamppost, as she spoke to a neighbour of my atypical appearance. Her little girl, Chrissie, had always been so thin and diminutive, "like a little doll", they used to say. She confided anxiously also to the neighbour the worry of the recently developed habit of biting my nails and also the unusual occurrence of my having wet the bed on my first night home. (Thankfully it was a unique happening because after John's hospital trauma and fractured skull, it remained a weakness of his for several years and I know how much washing my mother had to do in those days, with towelling nappies for the babies and most of all the difficulty of the boiling of clothes in a tin bath on the kitchen gas stove). The nail-biting I never did conquer in spite of my mother painting my nails with a bitter tincture,

Along with the nail-biting came the new propensity to cry at the slightest provocation if my feelings were hurt.

My mother fortunately never treated this as a fault but seemed to understand completely the reason for my tears. The other children often had to bear the brunt of her censure for making "Chrissie cry!" Myself I understand it now as the consequence of an unbearable separation from all those I loved at such an early age and if I am honest there was a strain of this melancholy that remained with me to this very day.

*

So, in instalments, we children returned to our parents and the new, copper-headed baby Tommy, in the new home in Vincent Street. The garden offered my dad some little continuity with his boyhood experiences on the farm in Ireland and in spite of his long hours in the factory, was soon busy planting the vegetables and potatoes and building a chicken house at the bottom, which overlooked the dirty River Sherbourne, polluted by the filthy overflow from the abattoir in York Street.

"Up the Top", where we were to play so much, rubble and shrapnel could be seen everywhere and as you approached the alley way that led into Thomas street you were confronted by overflowing dustbins and hills of garbage. The ground sloped down to that dismal river into which unspeakable bloody remains flowed from the slaughterhouse, through a long, underground tunnel.

Several of the braver boys (including of course my brother John) confessed to walking up that dark place even with animal entrails swirling at their feet. Only after several children, (my own brothers included) nearly drowned did the Council agree to erect a wall along the riverbank, but that was to be several years hence.

The house seemed so big! There were two rooms upstairs and two down. Apart from the brick toilet we had outside there was, two houses up, a brick-built wash house, to be used by all the mothers in the row. An enclosed copper vat would hold all the heavy washing to be done, water added and soap powder, and a small fire lit in the hearth below, to boil the water and so clean the clothes. For extra friction the women used wooden "dollies" to batter away the dirt, and in extremis, some clothes could be extricated to be rubbed vigorously on the washing board, the very same type used nowadays as a musical instrument! It must once have been a double washhouse but half of it had been blown away leaving a clumsy broken wall that jutted out in uneven steps – great for climbing on.

The house's garden seemed so long, leading down to the river. Dad, very quickly, barricaded away that danger by building his chicken pens to fill the gap. And the chickens? I was so proud! A custom at that time was for a rag and bone man to call out his business and children would run to parents for a few rags to give him (I never saw any one rich enough to have a spare bone that hadn't been boiled bare for soup!) In return the children were given little day-old yellow chicks. My dad had the knack. Whilst all the other children's chickens died, he would cosset ours in a little soft baby rug and put it in the black-leaded oven next to the fire with hobs used on either side to stand a saucepan of stew or soup to keep warm. The chickens invariably survived and so our family had extra eggs (one a week per person on the rations books would only give a Sunday morning treat!) More important it meant at Christmas there would be a big, hefty broiler that my father would strangle and put in a pot with carrots and onions and a big handful of barley and this we would enjoy as a feast on Christmas day. Until I was a grown up student I loved returning from midnight mass on a cold Christmas evening midnight to a big bowl of chicken and barley soup that my dad had made from boiling an old hen. In much later years I admit the hen was purchased at Coventry market! Dad though was like a child in his enthusiasm for celebrating Christmas! God bless the man!

I have never forgotten the flowers he grew as well as the vegetables. Where he got them is a mystery. There were tall hollyhocks of many shades of red and pink and big clumps of purple irises. His love for them was evidenced when ten years later, in 1952 when the family moved from Vincent Street to the large, Wimpey built, award-winning council estate in Tile Hill, the flowers came along with the few bits of furniture we possessed, (including, of course, the pictures of "Jesus Walking On the Waters" and "The Sacred

Heart of Mary", those precious heirlooms from Ireland.) The irises still bloom today over seventy years later.

*

From the earliest time I can remember there was a big wooden swing in our garden, attracting many of the children from around about. My dad built it and it was big. My mother uncharacteristically had loud and public disagreements with him about that swing, scared that one of the little ones might get a clonk on the head from an enthusiastic and careless big child, but he never relented, and time after time he mended it when it broke. I soon learned the knack of "working myself up" and later the art of leaping off in mid-air at the zenith of the swing, but nothing I think was as precious to me as time on late summer evenings when, with most of the family indoors, I would sneak into the garden to gently swing, dreamily and happily, listening perhaps to the sound of my father's flute from the kitchen, or maybe the group of his friends from Mayo, who came with violin and melodeon to make music with him.

Vincent Street was indeed a palace after Thomas Street. One room downstairs had an electric bulb. This was the front room where my parents slept on a bed-settee. This piece of furniture we rarely saw as a bed for it was always folded up to make a settee again by the time we were down and dressed for school. The little baby, who had slept with them, was now tucked into the pram or cradle pushed nearby. The back room or kitchen was lit with a gas mantle that lit with a pop and gave a deep yellow light. The two bedrooms, reached by a narrow curving set of stairs hidden behind a tall wooden door in the kitchen, relied on candles for light. In that same kitchen, dangling next to the gas mantle and even more fascinating, were long, yellow, twisting, sticky snakes of "Fly-catchers". They were always, even in winter I think, liberally festooned with dead or dying flies, the consequence of a poor rubbish disposal system and the chancellery, polluted River Sherbourne flowing nearby! For me they were scary and fascinating in equal measure, and regrettable only for the tears and anger they aroused in my poor mother and her despair at the never-ending battle, constantly replacing the fly papers and covering food against the onslaughts of those pernicious flies. (The flies and the bedbugs that seemed to inhabit the plaster on the walls nearly broke my mother's heart, much more than some of the physical tortures she had to endure, including the dreadful problems with her teeth and the persistent indigestion that gave her heartburn.) Each of the four rooms had a fireplace and although usually it was only the big black-lead range in the kitchen that contained a fire, in a bad winter or if one of us were ill, my dad would fill a flat shovel with hot coals from that main fire to take up to our bedroom. How magical it seemed like the flames from the small fire cast shadows on the bedroom walls.

We children slept in the two bedrooms upstairs in combinations that altered as yet another baby arrived in the family – number six, sturdy baby James! One enduring memory was of sharing a single bed with my sister Helen, in the back bedroom, the one overlooking the garden. It was lit by candles resting on a saucer on a wooden chair seat beside the bed. John slept on his own in a small bed under the window and often played tricks on us like when he tied a string from one bed leg to another so that when we came up to bed and the candle wasn't lit, we tripped over it! It was in that bed, probably before Teresa, baby number seven was conceived, that Helen and I shared a strange experience. The bedroom must have had a share of light from somewhere, because as we lay in bed we saw the life-size shadow of a lady walking the length of the bedroom wall, against which our bed was pushed. She seemed to be carrying a baby. She seemed to be almost shadow-like, but bright and in very clear silhouette, pressed against the wall. I remember we called down to our parents and mum and dad came up together, obviously keenly aware of the urgency in our call, because they would never have both responded so fast. By then the appearance had disappeared. We earnestly explained what we had seen, entirely without fear but with a desire to be believed. Our parents reassured us suggesting the possibility of it being our imagination. As they tucked us in again and started to descend the twisting stairs, I heard my mother whisper, "Do you think it was the Virgin Mary?" Not one of us ever spoke of it again. Strangely though, decades later when we met our cousin Nancy in America, four decades later she asked us this question, "And did you both really have a vision of the Blessed Virgin when you were children?" Helen immediately and strenuously denied it and no more was said. For years though I pondered it in my heart, torturing myself to find real-life explanations to account for it.

The front bedroom held a big four poster double bed with brass posts topped by lovely, golden, shiny metal balls. Here later the three boys would sleep, Michael, Thomas and James. Above the diminutive, iron fireplace hung the picture of Jesus walking on the waters in the midst of the storm. This amazing miracle may have been a timely inspiration for my poor parents, who amidst all the dolours of the continuing German raids and the struggles for food with the stringent rationing, and with three babies still under three years of age, were about to be faced with a challenge not much less daunting than that of walking the water was for Christ Himself. I mean no sacrilege or disrespect here. The dreaded scarlet fever was soon to present an unforgettable and terrifying challenge to these brave parents. Perhaps Our Lady really had paid a fleeting visit that night knowing the dreadful struggle and pain that lay ahead for John and Annie. Saint Mary was, after all, famous for turning up throughout history, when surely the heart was breaking – as she did at Knock in those famine years.

But back to Vincent street – a snug and lovely home for the next eleven years of my life. The front room doubled, or should I say trebled as parental bedroom; best room for special visitors like the priest; quiet room as a privilege for the ones keen to read and more rarely, receptacle for the long tin bath when, as we got older, we were considered to be in need of more detailed ablutions and certainly greater privacy. The kitchen of course was the hub, because the fire was there, and there too the food was cooked and eaten. It was also where one after the other of the children at bedtime were given their routine wash. It was also where my dad worked at the table mending shoes or making wooden toys or where mam in the daytime made the big soda cakes that we relished as a change from the bread. The kitchen had a black horse hair sofa, a wooden table pulled up in front of the coalhouse door, a few hard-backed kitchen chairs and to dry the clothes the old wooden "aunty", a wooden contraption of poles raised by pulley to dangle the clothes above our heads. Just as necessary was the big iron fire guard that encircled the fire to dry the most urgent garments like the babies' napkins and to protect the smaller children from falling into the fire – especially the crawling babies with their copious layers of flannel gowns and undergarments that could have incinerated a child in seconds (and indeed did, as was frequently reported in newspaper articles.)

This kitchen was where we really lived, played, ate, washed and prayed. It was there, at the table, I wrote my first little stories – excited beyond measure to see a pristine white page before me, dejected beyond measure to see the paltry offerings left by my pencil on the page, falling abysmally short of all my dreams and expectations. It was where also at the age of four years and eleven and three-quarter months, first of all the six children, I began to fall sick with that dreaded scarlet fever. And my parents were faced with the cruellest of challenges.

7

Scarlet Fever

"Death Comes Stalking Once Again"

It seemed the height of irony that as the bombing came to an end and at last we could sleep uninterrupted in our beds and the three baby O'Brien boys were plump and flourishing at one, two and three years of age, that fate should strike so cruel a blow.

As I mentioned before in those days, before the advent of antibiotics, scarlet fever was indeed a most serious illness, and often a killer. My mother knew this well for hadn't it killed her brother Tommy in Kiltimagh, at the age of five and wasn't it itself the reason why she was not at present in Philadelphia with her own mother and father and her brothers and sisters? And now her own little daughter, Annie Christina, on the cusp of being five, was diagnosed as having that same fever.

In my memory it must have started mildly because I recall being tucked in my parents' bed in the downstairs front room (a rare treat for a child who was ill) and being given a beautiful book for my fifth birthday on the seventh of October, the feast of the Holy Rosary. I hadn't yet started school because with the bombing of Saint Osburg's school entry had been delayed for all children and arrangements were being made to send the Catholic children to share the buildings of Saint John's school, with the "Protestants." It was situated at that time in Dover Street. How I had cried when John and Helen told me I couldn't after all go to the paradise, the real Saint Osburg's, they had repeatedly described for me, in anticipation of my fifth birthday. But, now in my illness, I had a beautiful book I could try to read. It was the story of the three little kittens who lost their mittens and my fever seemed more like a blessing because it gave me time to lie snugly in my parents' bed and study it to my heart's content. The three little kittens, first lost their mittens and went crying to their mother. She punished them by refusing them their pie! But then, oh happiness! They found their mittens, so mother gave them their pie! But then, oh dear! In eating it they soiled their mittens and again earned mother's disapproval! However, true to all human convictions of happy endings, love was restored when the three little kittens washed their mittens and proved to mother how good they really could be! Simplicity itself, but how I studied that birthday book as I snuggled, spoilt, in my parents' bed and watched the spots of fever gradually cover my little frame.

The fever though escalated rapidly. I was oblivious now to my parents' concern and was only told later of the two nights, when in fear of my life, the Parish priest of Saint Osburg's, Father Basil Griffin came and prayed at my bedside. Father Griffin was the twin brother of the then Cardinal of all England, Cardinal Bernard Griffin. (It was rumoured that Father Griffin had served in the war and been injured, because one of his eyes was glass.) He is engraved in my heart as the most holy and most caring of Parish priests. He was like a guardian angel to our family and although he had no time for gossip or chit-chat he knew us intimately and loved us without any outward show and often with a stern demeanour. In later years, on days of school reports, my mother would smarten us up, John, Helen and I, (and the others as they grew) to take us to the priest's humble house, which served as a presbytery, in Meridan street, Coundon, where he would carefully study our reports and advise us. He would bless our mother and praise her for her dedication and the good manners of her children. He knew of my father's devotion, seeing him sitting on the front pew at church on Sunday with all the little scrubbed faces beside him, precious pennies in the pocket for the collection and shiny, clean, Sunday shoes and tucked neatly behind the kneelers. On Saturday night, visiting our house you would see the shiny brushed shoes in ascending sizes ranked along the fender ready for the morning sortie.

    My mother said of Father Griffin, "He gave you Extreme Unction you know. That's what saved your life." Now with my knowledge of Catechesis I suspect it may not have been the sacrament for the dying, but prayers for a very sick child. What cannot be denied, however was that this good and humble priest stayed in our poor house for most of two nights and joined my parents in prayer for my life. The joy of the first signs of my recovery, or at least survival of the crisis, must have been tempered by the recognition a week later, that Helen had contracted the disease. In her case it seemed much milder so it came as a surprise when the medical authorities ordered that both Helen and myself be taken to an isolation hospital in case the four boys, John (seven), Michael (two and a half), Thomas (one and a half) and James, (three months), might contract it. It was on a Thursday we had to go, complete with gas masks, Helen's, black and grey, and grown up; mine red and green with a Donald Duck nose, for the toddlers, each in a brown cardboard box with a long strap to hang over the shoulder. Not that we were to use them then because Helen and I were carried to the ambulance.

Later my father told us that only two days afterwards all four boys had succumbed together to the fever. There seemed no point then of isolating them or treating them in hospital. It was a case of fight for survival. And to my parents fell the task of nursing three small boys under three, a spitfire of an eight year old whom neither asthma nor illness could subdue, but whom nevertheless was confined strictly to the house, and soon two shaky and tearful little girls, far from robust, and recently discharged from hospital. I clearly remember the day my father came to collect us. At the last minute they decided to keep Helen for another week as she still had an infected boil.

The nurse grumbled as she bundled me into my coat, "What on earth have you been teaching this child that she likes the Germans so much! Don't they come often enough without someone praying for them?" My father was dumbstruck! How was he to know that I had been totally in love with my next door neighbour's son of eleven, Gerry Mc Sorley, and when delirious or dreaming I had cried out loudly, "I want Gerry! I want Gerry!" What I didn't know as a child was that "Gerry" was the commonplace way then to refer contemptuously to the German bombers! Why I loved the real Gerry so much, I do not know, but I remember a great fondness for his black-haired pretty mother who taught me patiently to do French knitting before I became ill. Gerry was probably kind too and he became famous a few years later by earning a day's holiday from the mayor, for the whole of Saint Osburg's school for rescuing a child from drowning in the cursed river Sherbourne behind our houses. How strange it was when I met him again at the age of eighty, and he nearly ninety in my local church. I didn't tell my dad how ashamed I had been when they put me in a cot at the hospital. Fancy! As if I were a baby! Nor did I tell him of the horror of waking up each morning to a cot full of skin flakes and working frantically to brush them out onto the floor before the nurse found them and I was in trouble. (A natural consequence of the fever was the great dehydration of the skin and the consequent shedding of skin!) We did tell him laughing though of the daily pudding Helen and I received which we were sure was cheese, but turned out to be the most solid custard imaginable. It was lovely to see my dad. He put the obligatory gas mask container over my shoulder and I fell to the ground under the weight. I'm sure he must have carried me most of the way home and I wonder now whether he was reminded then of the night he had carried me home from the bombed shelter after they dug me from the rubble.

The long weeks of recovery are a haze in my memory. I think of all the sad crying of the babies with infected boils and sores, with abscesses in the ears, with discharging noses and who knows what other pains. Nurses came from time to time to lance a boil or dress a wound. Baby James languished weakly and hardly moved. John on the other hand was a hive of industry, usually keeping to his bedroom and making huge armies of imaginary soldiers by folding tiny pellets of paper and lining them into every kind of battle formation. I looked on enviously at his excited play battles but he guarded it all jealously and was lost in his own world.

No visitors. No visits, No school, No mass. Was there even an acknowledgement of Christmas passing? When would it end? It did though and some said it was a miracle that not one child was lost. But almost harder still came the six weeks of isolation and to mark the end of it the fumigators came, strange men in dark overalls to take our clothes and toys to burn in the garden, and then to spray the house and beds with foul-smelling chemicals.

But now at last we could resume everyday life. John remained as intrepid as ever and contended strongly to those other children capable of understanding, that it had been Chrissie who had brought the scarlet fever into the house, by playing in the dustbins near Thomas Street. There was some truth in what he said because I had played in the dustbins, so I tried to ignore his accusations. After all if even doctors had no knowledge of how the fever was transmitted and how it could be cured, why couldn't a bright boy of seven formulate his own theory? This is what my reason told me, but inside I was very hurt, because I loved him such a lot. And by then other things were on my mind and John's friendship was crucial. I was to start school at long last and though the beloved St Osburg's school was not yet restored from the bombing, John was to be responsible for taking me with Helen to the little school we were to share with the Church of England children – somehow or other!

8

The Beginning of the End of the War
"Got any gum Chum?"

The war was still on of course, but for us the worst was over. There were still the blackouts when in the evening, every vestige of household light was concealed by curtains or blankets from being seen outside in the street, in case there were any last forays of German bombers. The shelters still stood, sturdy and ready for occupancy, should there be such a raid and the dreaded sirens would wail. Rationing was still strictly in force and would continue to be so until 1948 – and some mystery foods, like bananas for instance, would wait for several years after that, before putting in an appearance. I remember my own utter disappointment to taste, at eleven years of age, the bland, banana fruit described to me as magical! My dad still worked long hours of overtime at the Dunlop factory making the rubber components that in later years were said to have to have caused bladder cancer in workers. My dad I know went several times to have some sort of bleeding warts removed from his bladder when he was in his fifties. Helen and I missed him a lot in the evenings and we often would prepare little letters of love for mam to give him when he came home. They were full of childish thanks to him for working so hard for us all.

The biggest change for all the children of the neighbourhood was the arrival in Coventry of American soldiers! After the Japanese attack on Pearl Harbour the Americans had joined in the war and now in Coventry, we were seeing evidence of this. Our excitement stemmed from confronting their handsome appearance, their superior size, and their smart uniforms. There was also their drawling good humour when talking with the children and the startling appearance of so much black skin. Most of all, though, was their seemingly inexhaustible supply of Wrigley's chewing gum, a luxury unknown to us at that time. It was commonplace for us children to greet a "Yank" with the phrase, "Got any gum chum?" and to follow them down the street or even to visit, on purpose, some park we knew they would frequent. Grey Friar's Green in town on the way to the station was a favourite. (That particular memory is burnt on my memory because it was sliding down the sloping roofs of concrete shelters there that rubbed a big hole in the backside of my white, silk bloomers purchased specially for my Holy Communion and all subsequent Sunday and Church Procession wear. I was devastated because although no one saw them they were the height of luxury for me and memories of such a special occasion! Maybe I was worried about being told off but if I were it would have made no difference, my remorse was so great.)

For some strange reason, the ruined silk bloomers and the American soldiers are permanently interwoven in my memories. It was very seldom that we were ever refused our requests for gum – even if we received only one strip from the packs of five. In the presence of rationing and few sweets it was like manna from heaven! Perhaps we picked up too, in some subliminal way, that these kind men were indeed our saviours, for it was to send bombing missions over to German cities and bring an end to war that these troops were stationed here.

You may remember my writing earlier in my story of how my mother's mother, Bridget, had left Ireland in 1915 to join her husband in Philadelphia, taking Mum's brother John with her and leaving little Annie behind because she had scarlet fever. Annie, you will remember was my mother's name. Once reunited with her husband Michael in Philly, Bridget had had four more children, Mary, Michael Junior (or Michael Sonny as he was always known), Martin and Alice. Now in 1947, grown to be men, mother's three brothers, John, Michael Sonny and Martin, had all been conscripted into the USA army to join the allies and fight in earnest against the German Forces. So, unknown to us children at the time, we had three of our closest relatives, three uncles, fighting for us against the Germans.

The youngest uncle Martin was in Iceland, working they said as an air-mechanic helping to maintain and mend the vehicles of war. Little was ever spoken of him except that he adapted very badly to Civvy life after the war and died very young of cancer of the spine and ribs. This all seems hard to understand because he was reputed to have had outstanding athletic ability and was a member of the Greenland Base Command Basketball team that were runners up in the North Atlantic Title 1945. He had also been decorated, they said at his funeral, with a Good Conduct Medal, The American Campaign Medal, The European African Middle Eastern Campaign Medal and the World War II Victory Medal. It remains a mystery what happened to him when he left the army. There seems to have been some element of shame attached that relatives refused to discuss.

Anyway, before going to Iceland whilst training on the Airplane mechanic's course he had written to my mother in Coventry, whom of course he had never seen.

"Dear sister Annie. My name is Martin Mullaney," he wrote, "and I am your youngest brother. As you might know I am twenty-two years of age....(after queries about her well-being and that of her family)... I want you to know that my one big ambition is to see you face to face. And when I set out to do something, I usually accomplish it. So some day we have a date and I hope you won't stand me up on it!" My mother kept this letter until she died.

Today I console myself that in a land warmer than Iceland this gentle-hearted young man, uncle Martin, is able to fulfil his ambition to his heart's content, to see his sister face-to-face and that Annie, my mum, can be together again with him and all those dear relatives she never knew in her life-time. Most especially her father. Uncle John, the eldest brother, meanwhile was fighting in India but what happened there no one ever knew, because until the day he died he refused to speak of it or of any wartime experience. His wife and children knew better than to ask him about it. Poor Uncle John, he was always a tender one. (Now as an adult myself and having read so much of the experiences of ex-soldiers from World War II, I realise that Uncle John was in no way unusual in being unable speak again of what must have been intolerable traumas.)

When he had the chance many, many years later to visit my mum in England he refused to come to Coventry, so fearful was he of seeing some of the war damage and being reminded of what his sister and her family had suffered. Instead he met with her in Kiltimagh, near their birthplace. (My aunt Alice later told me that after his discharge from the army and his marriage to the ebullient and lovely Yolanda from Italy, John's early married life, whilst working as a Civil servant, was devoted to the purchasing of two homes – one for his own family, when he had one, and one for that of his sister Annie in Coventry, whom he planned to move to Philadelphia, with her family). Apparently, he had very strong memories of his childhood in Kiltimagh and he recalled clearly the pain of the separation when his sister was left behind as he and his mother had left for America. Uncle John's plan for my mother never came to fruition. (If it had, I wouldn't be sitting here now writing these words!)

His second child, Patsy was born with a severe disability and he sold the second home he had bought for our family, to pay astronomic fees for various, and mostly unsuccessful health procedures and operations. Gone were the hopes, in Uncle John's mind of shipping the entire O'Brien family from Coventry to Philadelphia! No chance now to assuage that relentless guilt that so often torments those deemed more fortunate. He had secured a good job in the Civil Service and by most people's standards was financially secure.

As for Uncle Michael, he was a bombardier stationed in England about thirty miles from Coventry. Even my mother was ignorant of all these things. She had never set eyes on either her father or her four siblings born in America anyway, and John she only remembered from the parting scene at the railway station when he was a little child of seven. I recap only to recount this little tale – told to us so many times by my mother – for the utter miracle of it! She was sitting by the coal fire, she said, with all six of us asleep upstairs in bed (three little boys in the big bed in the front bedroom, me and Helen in our single bed by the inside wall and John in a little bed on his own just a stride away in the back bedroom.) She was busy making a peg rug from strips of cloth she had cut from old clothes (the most luxurious form of floor covering then) and waiting for my dad to come home from his long hours of work in the factory. A knock came to the front door. The blackout was strict, so she dared not peek out through the curtains, and even if she did Vincent street itself, without street lighting, was as black as a grave. "Who is it?" she asked, in fear.

"Only your brother!" came the reply in a thick American accent.

My mother was always confused telling us the next bit. She knew straight away it was true, that it really was her brother, and when she opened the door to rush him into the house from the darkness, she recognised him as related, by the red hair and wide cheekbones, even though his peaked cap slanted forward on his brow. It was Michael, her younger brother, and she had never seen him before. He had only a day's leave from the air force to stay with our family. He was terribly tired and later he squeezed into the big double bed upstairs to sleep with the three little boys, Mick, Tom, and Jim. Against the cold he put his big trench coat on the bed to cover them and I remember that finely-made coat, heavy and warm being put on many a bed for the remainder of my childhood because Uncle Michael left it behind for us and said he'd get a replacement by swapping some ammunition. What passed between the brother and sister, what tears were shed, what questions asked, what promises made or messages sent, we were never to know. Nor the shock my father received when he arrived home at 11 O'clock at night, to find his wife, in her very own kitchen, sitting snugly with a handsome, young American soldier!

Uncle Michael had a dangerous job, flying sorties

over Germany and when he died it was revealed in a newspaper report that he had flown many more than the required number, well over thirty, and been given a prestigious award. I read later that it was the Distinguished Flying Cross Medal. His big present for us all when we greeted him in the morning was a big fat rabbit! (dead of course and shot through the head). He'd swapped that too, he told us, with a fellow crew-man, for some of his rifle ammunition and he must have known how precious it was for us to be able to have a big rabbit stew when meat was so scarce. What he didn't tell us was that the lack of rifle ammunition could have cost him his life, if it had caused him to be shot down over Germany without the means of redress. It had had happened to so many of his friends

One of his crew mates at Michael's funeral submitted an account of one of their sorties to make a raid on Kiel from their English base. He wanted people to understand the perils of life as a bombardier. It was on the way home from a successful mission when disaster struck and their plane "the Liberator" was left with only one engine to cross the North Sea and negotiate a landing. His account made the hairs on the back of my neck stand on end and I then began to have a small grasp of what these American soldiers had suffered for us and of course our debt to them, and Uncle Michael in particular. Along with his fine coat, with his fat rabbit, Uncle Michael gave my mother also some undefinable present – a sense of love, of pride, of belonging, of really and truly having a family, of being sought out and not left behind to weep with the emptiness within. In no small measure his visit had begun to heal the desperate void in her heart torn from her that day at Kiltimagh station as the train engines screamed. And who knows, perhaps he had planted the seed of hope that one day she would be united again with her family?

And so with the advent of the Americans the war did seem to be ending. The prosaics of life began again to reassert themselves. How to use that bright yellow powder to make scrambled egg. How to get the children to swallow that sickly cod liver oil so necessary to escape rickets. How to keep the house warm. How to make the best use of the Care parcels that started to come regularly from the relatives in the United States – sometimes food, sometimes clothes or baby items. Once even, at Christmas, a six-pound box of sweets! Those sweets were probably made to last until the following Easter, because I never remember being given more than one in a day.

Without wireless and national newspapers, we children were cocooned from the terrifying happenings of the last months of the war where in so many parts of the globe satanic evils were being revealed, and certainly I have no memory of my parents or visitors discussing it. A few local events impinged on our consciousness as having some connection. A young neighbour, with two young children, shortly after his discharge from the army was found hanging from the overhead cistern of one of the outside lavatories, The horror of his death was somehow exacerbated by the shame of the place where it had occurred. Another neighbour was demobbed early too. He had been discharged because of a bullet wound to his foot. I heard of the cruel, circulating rumours that he was a coward who had injured himself on purpose to escape from the fighting,

I felt very sorry for him because he gave all of us children the most amazing dark, dark chocolate that was inches thick and so hard you had to gnaw at it. They said it was army issue chocolate, jam-packed with calories to sustain you when you were up against it! He also had some magical toys – a sort of bat you held in your hand which had little pigeons standing on it and when you moved the pigeons would all bow their heads and pick at the bat as if feeding. It was worked by strings attached to a weight dangling beneath. I hope that poor soldier got some consolation from all our fascinated attention and gratitude to make up for the malice that enshrouded him.

War though, in my mind took a hugely diminished importance because the day was finally at hand when my health was sufficiently recovered from the fever and my city barely recovered from the very worst of the bombing to enable a keen and excited five year old to begin her formal education.

9

Early School Days
"Saint Ossie's at Last – Hurrah!"

I was to be late starting school because of the Scarlet Fever, but also because time was needed to prepare the Anglican school of Saint John's, allocated for our education until the Catholic St. Osburg's school was repaired. I had had such wonderful dreams of school from all the tales told to me by John and Helen and how disappointing it was now to be crammed into quite another school, with neither staff nor equipment to cope with us.

There was no integration. Whilst the Protestant children (Proddy Dogs) went in for a lesson, the Catholics (Catty Cats) stood in the playground and counted to a hundred – again and again. When the hour was up the Protestant children came out to count and the Catholic children went in. This was repeated throughout the day. I remember only two lessons. One was to write "The cat sat on the mat" with chalk on a little square slate, and then rub it out with a little square duster. The other lesson I usually passed under the long school bench weeping, because try as might I could not learn to knit. A particular teacher terrified me and at night when I said my prayers, I thanked God that she mainly taught the big children – though I was still very worried that John might suffer at her hands. I never remember seeing a book, but fortunately Helen and John were allowed to take me with them on their weekly excursions to the public lending library in Earlsdon. Here, I studied books to my heart's content. I wasn't allowed to borrow books myself because I was not yet seven, the official age then for joining the library and borrowing two books for two weeks, but with a child's logic I prepared for that wonderful time by hiding my favourite books carefully behind all the other books on the shelf. Each week my first task on arriving at the library was to search out the books I had hidden so carefully the previous week, only to face failure! Some assiduous librarian had discovered my treasure and restored the books to their rightful place. In spite of the disappointment I persisted, quite sure that one day I would succeed!

  Real life seemed to begin with our return to the partially restored St. Osburg's. Now we could stay in the classroom all day long except for playtime and a military form of P.E. in the playground. Neither did we have Proddy Dog children calling us names and telling us to find our own school. We stretched arms and jumped on the spot like proper little soldiers and with what discipline we lined up in classes at the end of playtimes, in perfectly straight lines with arms extended to rest on the shoulders of the child in front! Any sergeant major would have been pleased with his battalion! The lines were long because there were usually about sixty children in each class and talking was strictly forbidden. Any blatant, or even secretive, breach of this rule resulted in a directive to join the caning queue outside the headmaster's study, where one or two swipes were administered, from a long thin cane, with varying degrees of vehemence assessed easily by the strength of the whoosh, the size of the red welt across the palm of the hand, or more plainly still by the sight of the tears that trickled down even the toughest cheeks.

It broke my heart to see how often John was selected for punishment – so much so that it became the headmaster's great joke to the school, that "There will be pink elephants walking down the road in striped pyjamas on the day that John O' Brien doesn't talk in line." Helen on the contrary was good or careful and was never singled out for disgrace, and since I was small my misdemeanours were usually rewarded with a resounding slap on the top of my thigh, from a specially garbed black-leathered glove worn by the infant teacher. On the single occasion I was sent for caning to the headmaster, still short of seven, I remember standing at the end of a long line of reprobate boys, (not John on this day) all of them much bigger than me and some even approaching fourteen, the age then to leave school, don long trousers and start work. With terror I watched as one by one the boys met their fate. Oh what spitting on hands, jiggling round in agony, bending double with hands clutched between thighs! But now it was my turn – my hand had to be extended. I closed my eyes. At first there was a slight whoosh, then a pause before the sharp cane descended gently on to my hand. A pause of wonder as if at a miracle, and then the other hand was brushed. Of course, I cried whether from mortification or relief I had no idea. We were dismissed and I never talked in line again!

These might seem off-putting incidents but school nevertheless, once safe in St. Osburg's, was a haven. We could go into church once a week for mass and every Friday for Benediction after school and we could see dear Father Griffin and have little talks from him when he visited the school. He never knew our names. All the girls were Angelina – Angelina with the plaits, big Angelina, Angelina with the red hair and so on. The same rule was applied to the boys, but they were the infinite variety of Georges! We really and truly belonged once we were in St.Osburg's! In huge classes of nearly sixty we made friends and learned. I always found a seat as near the front as possible – it was to be four years before my eyes were tested and I was found to be seriously short-sighted. I've no idea how I learned to read but I did in a trice and in no time my favourite pastime was to write stories and my addiction was to read.

I would write stories everywhere. Once sitting on the doorstep in the sun writing I was approached by a passing man to ask what I was doing. When I told him, he glanced at my efforts and said for such work I definitely deserved payment. He gave me a sixpenny piece. That was like the equivalent of a pound in today's money. Running in to show my mother she said to me quite sternly, "You must remember this day. It's the first time you have earned money by your very own work." I felt very proud when she said this and never did forget it.

One memory from school, and now it seems very narcissistic, was overhearing two teachers talking. They didn't know I was there. One suddenly began reading a child's writing and as she read I recognised the words of my latest story about Little Tom Thumb. She read, "Down, down, down, he fell this little chap, from the horse's mane." "How expressive!" she added "for a little child."

The strange thing was that the teachers didn't know that I was listening, I can't remember them mentioning my name and later I was never praised for any achievement. I realise now, only after a lifetime of teaching, that in some way although teachers obviously recognised achievement (I was only just six at that time), they did not indulge in huge praise for their pupils but left them in the dignity of their own development, without being singled out, minutely examined or made to feel different and self-conscious. That privacy in the development of my thought and skills, I will always be grateful for. Perhaps my character benefited too in not being encouraged to think I was better than anyone else.

But apart from the reading, writing and arithmetic skills my first two years at school were important because I was to develop in my religious or spiritual life. My faith was the air that surrounded me at home, whether it was the mass attended on Sunday with my father, the Benediction on Sunday afternoon with Helen and John and dad too (sometimes), or whether it was the indispensable, nightly rosary recited on our knees before bed. It was also in the words and pious ejaculations of my parents, my mother, in her "God willing!", "Please Gods!", "God forgive me!" or at times of crisis, "Jesus, Mary and Joseph, help us." with the fervour of hope that brought tears to your eyes. One typical situation might have been when baby fell on his head – or some similar disaster.

It seemed to us children, that as well as having a mother and father looking after us, there was, in fact God – as another member of the family, and one in a very senior and helpful position! I suppose with none of us ever having a grandparent or even an aunt, uncle or cousin around, it seemed only to be expected that God would step in to fill the gap! It had its humorous side too because my mother described to me how once when she was worn out with the racket of the three little boys, in desperation she had cried out, "My dear God can I not have a bit of peace!"

James quite forward talking then, only two, turned to her and said, "You can have a little bit of my piece!" handing her the piece of bread and butter she had just given the naughty boys to quieten them down! Another incident I clearly remember myself because it made me laugh a lot much later. Again, in desperation, with the squabbles and uproar of a wet afternoon indoors, my mother complained, "God forgive me for being so impatient! Shouldn't I be like God's mother herself all peaceful and calm! .... But then", and she paused, "..she didn't have a crowd like you to look after – she had only one little fellow to look after and I'm sure he was a good little mite!" I could imagine Our Lady smiling in sympathy at such honesty!

School gave me the chance to read about my faith, largely in the form of countless books giving the lives of saints. They lay in the big private reading cupboard, at the front of our classroom, near the huge black metal furnace that kept the classroom warm and let out a constant gentle trickle of smoke. These books were inauspicious in appearance, with the quality almost of tissue paper, with covers made of parcel wrapping paper and without a picture in sight! Every chance I got, having finished my maths or my composition, I would dive into the reading cupboard and read voraciously. How I loved the saints! From every country and every century, although I didn't know that then. I was fired by their virtues, their courage, their love, and devotion. They lived lives that were special and holy and lovely and I became quite sure that that was the only true vocation to have, to be a saint, to learn to be good and to love God with all your soul. We learned the penny catechism too off by heart and it all made perfect sense. Catechism! What a perfect way to present such complex ideas to a young child whose very life till the age of five, consists in asking questions! (To many an adult too, who decades later might find themselves asking the same existential questions!)

> "Who made you?"
> "God made you."
> "Why did God make you?"
> "God made me to love Him and serve Him in this life and to be happy with Him for ever in the next."

Any philosopher confronting the existential questions of life would do well to consult the penny catechism! And any teacher of social and ethical development would be much helped by an examination of the concepts outlined in the "Fruits of the Holy Spirit" or the section on "Corporal and Spiritual works of mercy"!

The most momentous event though, of these two years was to prepare for Holy Communion, the sacrament a Catholic receives after Baptism and Confession. Now I was not only to enter more closely into the Church and God's family, but I would know about it! I have often wondered since, why and how a child can be expected to grasp the full significance of this most holy and momentous Sacrament. To receive, in the form of a little host of unleavened bread, the very body and blood of Our Lord and Saviour, Jesus Christ the Son of God, who had died for us on a cross, to open the gates of heaven, closed so long ago by the sin of

Adam, so that we could reach that destiny he had planned for us at our very creation – how can that miracle be understood by a child?

Once, when James was nearly two and still couldn't walk at all after suffering the scarlet fever, he had pulled himself up by my father's boot as we knelt together one evening, as a family, saying the rosary. He started to walk, and we children were amazed at the suddenness of it. We thought it was a miracle. If a rosary could make a miracle surely, in mass itself, why should it be strange to have the miracle of the Blessed Eucharist? What magic, what wonder, what internal perfection could be within reach if we could receive the Blessed Sacrament? Our little souls had already been described to us by our teachers as "as white as the wool of little gambolling lambs in Springtime", after we went to confession for the first time, or "as bright as the very star that shone over the stable of the Christ child on that first Christmas morning". Strange as it seems we were fully convinced of the reality of the inner life and had an early concept of the theological meaning of grace.

How lovely, how entrancing was the service of mass to a child. The priest was there with vestments now green, now red, now yellow, or white or now deep purple, as in Lent. There was even pink for Laetare Sunday (fourth Sunday celebration in the frugal six weeks of Lent). In those convoluted robes made from silk or satin or shiny damask, the priest walked down the aisle like a prince, followed by his train of young altar servers dressed in their black robes, covered by white lace-trimmed surplices. The altar was fringed with exquisite lace, hand-made they said by the nuns. The golden tabernacle stood in the centre, its central, mysterious door opening with a golden key to divulge the precious chalice. Candles burned everywhere with a golden glow and incense filled the air from swinging censors. Words in Latin, dignified and sonorous, were enunciated in loud and reverent tones over the cup that held the unconsecrated hosts. The priest elevated the host as heads lifted first to adore and then to bow in prayer as the bread was transformed into the body of Christ. Similarly, with the consecration of the wine.

The sacrifice of Calvary was re-enacted, and the promise of Redemption was fulfilled. Mass continued as people knelt, stood, prayed or sang according to the dictates of the service. It fascinated me always how, on entering Church, suddenly the relationships between people faded away as each member of the congregation focussed all his attention on the presence of Our Dear Lord on the altar.

"I will look now, with all my heart and soul and will. I will look now and see what is not there. With my eyes I will drink in this sight. I will drink it into my very being. I will drink in so much more than this sight. And it will still be there, in all its grandeur and inaccessibility so I will look again and drink again in a delight that has no satiety."

Such were the thoughts that went through so many

heads. And for me to receive Holy Communion as a little child of six and three quarters was to be a culmination of all these other intimations of a blissful union with Jesus, the one who loved us so dearly.

10

Holy Communion and the Arrival of Baby Teresa
"I Once had a Sweet Little Doll Dears"

Then, in 1944, as now, more than seventy years later, little girls wore white dresses for Holy Communion and little white veils. By this sacrament of the Eucharist, they were to become the true brides of Christ, and as white inside and out as the driven snow. So, the teacher taught, and I believed – though I wasn't very sure why driven snow should be whiter than ordinary snow.

I was well aware that my dress was not so special. It had been worn by my sister Helen before me and was a somewhat dingy, clingy crepe, which is not a good material to wear if you are painfully thin.

"Thank God at least it has long sleeves," my mother comforted me, "and at least it will cover the desperate, thin arms on you!" And she added in great sadness, "I'm sure people will think I don't feed you enough." For in normal, everyday life she never let me go out without a cardigan for fear my thinness would be revealed! The wreath for my veil was a collar from another white dress, cleverly adapted to look a bit more special than a pair of hair clips. I didn't mind all this, I just wanted so much to go to Communion and receive Our Blessed Lord, to be full of grace, to shine and to be holy – just like a saint. I had read so many of the lives of saints and how I wished to emulate them. For me this was the first step on that road to being joined truly to Our Lord.

The Sacrament was to take place in Saint Osburg's Church, (the mother church of Coventry and the first to be built in the city after the act for the Emancipation of Catholics. This was in 1845. A small chapel had been built on the same site at the top of Hill Street, fifty years earlier and before that Catholics in the city would walk the eight miles to Wappenbury to celebrate mass. Do you remember I reported how the whole roof of this church was blown off on the night of the Great Blitz, the same night as the Saint Michael's Cathedral was almost razed to the ground? Now, however the roof was roughly repaired, and it was business as usual with Church liturgy. The priest giving us the Sacrament would be Father Basil Griffin, who knew me well. Remember he was the one who had prayed at my bedside on two consecutive nights when I was dying of Scarlet Fever at the age of five, but he only ever addressed me as "Angelina with the red hair". My teachers and all my little friends would surround me on every side. My parents and all my siblings would be there in the church, even James at two and a half and walking at last. How proud they would be of me; how proud I would be of them! How happy I would be! But here my memory grows dim. Everything was to change. "The best laid schemes of mice and men" would truly go astray!

Was it in the early morning of that special day,

awake early and eager to get dressed, (my mum had even bought me brand new white silk bloomers, which would slightly compensate for the second-hand dress!) that I knew something was wrong. I learned, to my utter amazement, that in the night my little sister Teresa had inconveniently entered the world. In the front room of our four-roomed house in Vincent street, in the marital bed we rarely saw extended, (but only in the shape of a sofa, for it was indeed a bed-settee), in the presence of some plump, local woman, deemed mid-wife, another little O'Brien had entered the world. It was, after three boys, another little red-headed girl. On this day, of all days, this precious, precious day, of my first Holy Communion, 10th June 1944!

Shouldn't I have been utterly delighted that God had sent me such a beautiful present to celebrate my entry into the life of Christ? Not so! Years later as adults, in the morphine-flavoured days of this same Teresa's final illness from ovarian cancer, when she was only forty one, we women of the family, Helen and mum, and Margaret and me, gathered with Teresa, as we did every evening in the last few weeks of her life, until she was too frail to rise from her bed. My dad and the brothers would have absented themselves for a consoling pint, knowing their women's need for reminiscence. We would gather in front of the live fire, at the family house in Wheate Croft, Tile Hill to recall childhood memories, and one evening, Helen reminded her that her birth had actually coincided with the Sunday of my

Holy Communion. At this Teresa turned so gently to me and said with a smile, "You must have hated me then!" Because she knew of course, that with all the activity in the household, only Helen would have been free to accompany me in my day of joy to be a witness to this great, madly anticipated event. Sweet Teresa, with her great empathy, divined, even when close to death, the pain that had afflicted me then at the age of six and a half.

At the altar rails though, I knelt with great love and piety. I welcomed Jesus into my soul. Helen knelt somewhere far behind me but there was a stone in my heart that I couldn't smile with joy to my dear mother and father and see their pride in me. Afterwards at the Communion breakfast, (in these days of rationing we had the rare luxury of a boiled egg with bread and butter) as I ate I felt like swords the pitying glances of the gossiping women who served us and who examined with their eyes, my poor clothes, having expert knowledge of their origins and who, as they whispered together, were swift to calculate the numbers and ages of all the other children in my family, and no doubt with relish, anticipated the likelihood of future additions, judging from the youth and beauty of my mother.

*

Teresa though, as a baby is very dim in my recollection, which is strange. For a start she was a girl, succeeding three noisy little boys. Also, she had red hair like me but whereas mine was a duller auburn and Tom's a rich copper, she had hair that was truly red and very thick and beautiful as she grew.

And yet I can't remember being deeply involved with her as a baby, but instead jumped into a world of my own obsessions – the first was an intense fixation on a motherhood of my own, via any dolls I could find. The second, which I will describe in another chapter, an incurable compulsion to read, and read and read, and this, whatever I could get my hands on. I remember so clearly the long days spent dressing and undressing any poor doll we could find. One came from a friend of my parents who had won it in a raffle, and since there was only one doll, Helen and I shared it between us, taking turns to count to twenty, we held it lovingly in the single bed we slept in. It was made from a brown stocking but had a sweet little plaster face. My mother, in this activity, sensing my deep even desperate involvement, completely exceeded my expectations. She let me have some of baby Teresa's clothes – the back flannel, the vest, the liberty bodice, the long gown and of course the bulky, terry napkins with their big safety pins. How many clothes a baby wore in those days and how much washing they produced! How I loved to dress my doll, and swaddle it in a sheet or blanket as I saw my mother do and how complete was my joy when she let me borrow her own best cream Winceyette nightie to wear. Nothing could be more beautiful than the two blue roses embroidered on the breasts.

  I could not understand how a mother could be so generous and kind! In a fantasy world I dressed in the lovely nightie like a queen and cared for my child. It had taken so many weeks for me to summon up the courage to ask mum if I could borrow her lovely nightie and yet she agreed without demur. This was one of my mother's greatest gifts to me I often think that she was so sensitive to the reality and importance of my inner life and was humble in her respect and deference to it. She gave me the certainty, that always in my heart, unspoken and unexamined by others, I could think and hope and dream and live my very private life with dignity and without intrusion.

My love of dolls must have been well-known because my little friend, Bernadette had an older sister who noticed my fascination and offered to let me borrow her very own doll, (China, not rag) for a whole weekend. I remember I took it everywhere with me even to the park, the Sandpit, by name – still there today next to the Butt's arena, but without the splendid sandpit! But here comes the sadness. One of those moments in a child's life that carve an indelible regret on the soul. As Helen and a friend returned from the park with me and me hugging the precious doll, we passed a public toilet which we all had great need of, having played out for hours. I had a dilemma. I needed the toilet so badly! But how could I possibly take such a beautiful doll into the dark and smelly interior of that toilet. "I know," I thought, "I'll just sit little dolly on the grass verge outside and then she'll be so nice and clean".

Imagine the pain when I came out again to grasp my treasure, to find it had gone! My heart was broken! It was my fault! And not only had I lost the precious doll, but it wasn't even mine to lose and Bernadette's sister would never forgive me! I cried many tears. I never knew exactly how news of the loss was either given or received, but I do remember Bernadette later confiding in me that her sister, (Mary, I now recall), had intended to give me the doll, since I loved it so dearly, to keep forever! Now this couldn't happen. I had lost my little doll twice. A double grief! Years later I encountered the poem "The lost Doll" and cried again as I copied it and learnt it by heart. Of course, I will include all the words in my little epilogue at the end of my story, because it so vividly spoke to my heart.

> *I once had a sweet little doll, dears the prettiest doll in the world........*
> *But I lost my sweet little doll, dears, as I played on the heath one day.......*
> *Though I cried for her more than a week, dears I never could find where she lay.*

The obsession with dolls persisted for many years, so much so that when my twelfth birthday was approaching and I was excelling in Latin and maths at Grammar school, as well as being the best high-jumper in my class, I told my mother in strictest confidence, that I had seen the most beautiful small doll in Woolworth's for only half a crown and could I have it for my birthday – but not to tell anyone. Without a sign of surprise my mother told me that was a good idea and bought it for me. No one ever knew of the clandestine transaction and as far as I know the doll was hidden away and never again saw the light of day! It had still been something of great importance to me. It was surely evidence too of that almost preternatural understanding and sensitivity shown by my mother to my many, many needs.

11
Passion for the Written Word
"Realms of Gold"

My other passion wasn't so well received as had been my passion for dolls. This was my passion for reading. From the earliest memory of "The cat sat on the mat," (written on a small black slate with a little piece of chalk) reading of the most complex nature seemed to be a natural and easy progression. I can't remember any phonetics, alphabet learning, word recognition or any such games. What seemed always of importance was what was told in the reading and what was its relevance to my life, my hopes, my dreams. In each class room at our school, (now Saint Osburg's, restored and repaired as was the Church, after the bombing) there was always the cupboard of "silent readers" – a heap of picture-less, rather tatty, close-printed books of every level, usually consisting of fairy tales, legends, myths, fables, poetry and the many, many lives of the saints. These last were my joy. I have mentioned them already in reference to my early spiritual development. There were saints of every age in history and from every land, so as well as receiving an assortment of laudable role models, (as well as the daubings of a dubious piety sometimes), I gleaned a smattering of history, out-of-date geography and a truly fascinating vocabulary. I gravitated here at every opportunity, when my maths was complete, or my story written.

I very soon had devoured the few books we had in the house. Remember, everything in our house in Vincent street had been fumigated or burnt after our illness with scarlet fever, but I doubt there had ever been many books to start with. The long and dramatic ballads that my father recited to us at bedtime were firmly in his memory, never taken from a book. We nodded off to the fair maiden cast up on the deserted beach on Norman's Woe, after the "Wreck of the Hesperus" (by Longfellow); or we shed tears of sympathy as Lord Ullin cried,

My daughter, Oh my Daughter.......as........
The waters wide went o'er his child,
And he was left lamenting!
(by Thomas Campbell)

(It was his own fault really. If he had let her marry her brave chieftain, they wouldn't have had to flee on horseback together and try to escape across the loch on such a stormy night! You must read it for yourself!)

Dad's repertoire was small, but huge in sorrow and drama! The melodic rendering of his recitation was only surpassed by the emotional charge of the endless tunes he played on his tin whistle. But how it instilled in us a love for poetry of all kinds. There were only three whole books as far as I can remember in the house, and all of them were in the original text. No amended or abridged versions in those days. No sanitising of extremities to suit the imagined sensibilities of children as is the modern Disney vogue. Only today I thought of my first reading of the original of Hans Christian Anderson tales and how I had been profoundly moved to think of the little mermaid being prepared to endure a lifetime of the pain of walking on knives in order to gain the love of her prince. I thought what a wonderful metaphor for true love, whether of man or God – the readiness to suffer for it. (I think the thoughts were prompted by the stabbing pain I was getting from a back strain at the time – in which case it seemed very unlikely I had much capacity for true love!)

The books then in our house were "Treasure Island" by Robert Louis Stevenson, "Robinson Crusoe" by Daniel Defoe and a miniature but complete copy of "Pilgrim's Progress" by John Bunyan. It was this last work that made the deepest impression on me. In "Pilgrim's Progress" I grasped and always remembered the concept of life as a journey and a struggle, fraught with obstacles and dangers, with the battle against self and sin, the most terrible of all. Naturally, this understanding would reinforce much of my learning from my religious education lessons, and also the lived philosophy of my parents, unarticulated usually, but probably more powerful because of that.

But in one clear verse I found expressed the answer

that makes it possible for the soul to continue and persevere in this dangerous battle and never sink into the slough of despair. For me, at age seven, this was a moment of startling illumination. It was of course, as every Christian knows, the revelation that every sinner (and hence every man) should remember, the hope and promise for each soul, of redemption and salvation, wrought by the crucifixion of Jesus Christ, Our Lord. To this day I remember the words of that verse that Bunyan puts into the mouth of the eponymous pilgrim, Christian. Did I learn it once at seven or eight or nine years of age? Or was it read and reread when books were in such short supply, and thus it etched itself indelibly on my mind? Did I copy the words carefully in my best handwriting as I later loved to do with my favourite poems? I can't remember exactly what the reason was, but from earliest childhood I remembered exactly how it goes. There was never a time, as there was with most other poems, that I forgot a few words and had to look it up. It is Christian, the pilgrim, representing Everyman, who speaks the words:

> *Far have I come, laden with my sin,*
> *Nor could ought ease me of the grief that I was in,*
> *Till I came hither. What place is this?*
> *Must here be the beginning of my bliss?*
> *Must here the burden fall from my back?*
> *Must here the strings that bound it to me crack?*

> *Blest cross! Blest sepulchre!*
> *Blest ever be,*
> *The man who there was put to death for me.*

This must have been one of the deepest of my reading insights, for it taught me that someone else, and so often in my experience, voiced in the words of a poem, can pose and answer one of the most profound spiritual questions asked by a human heart. I heard the same sentiment expressed by Hector in the play "History Boys" by Alan Bennet when considering sacrilegious thought; that it can often be a quotation from a poem that contributes more strongly to spiritual development than any biblical reference. From this keen observation, what I learned from this quotation is that every human being sins and carries the weight of their guilt for that sin, often suffering greatly because their responsibility for it cannot be denied. And with it the knowledge that cannot be evaded, as a result of that sin, something has irrevocably been damaged. However, God in his mercy did not leave humans to their great suffering and culpability but gave his only son Jesus Christ to die on the cross in atonement for all of mankind. To realise this is to experience the over-powering gratitude that Christian felt,

> *Blest ever be,*
> *The man that there was put to death for me!*

Those novels, "Treasure Island" and "Robinson Crusoe" also became close companions too and had the added merit of being so long you could read them again and again and never get bored. The discussion of my passion for books would not be complete without mentioning the importance of the library in Earlsdon. This was the obligatory and longed for rendezvous, for John, Helen and me, every Saturday, after our similarly obligatory visit in the morning, to Saint Osburg's church for weekly Confessions. I think I've mentioned this before and now at seven I was old enough to become a proper member and have an inexhaustible source of new books. The journey to the library meant navigating several road crossings, but after the war, cars and petrol were in short supply and posed little danger. I remember being firmly convinced that inside the rare cars we saw, there must have been a race of truly superior human beings of quite extraordinary sensitivity and refinement. Many years later I rather despised myself for having such a mistaken and even grovelling view of class differences, but it occurred to me once as a teenager, that maybe this wasn't such a strange idea, but was perhaps the result of an inborn conviction I held in man's perfectibility – but that I had confused it in my naivety, with material advancement! (It reminded me of the similar experience I had as a fifteen year old cyclist when, with my friends Pauline, Anne and Hilary, we first cycled to Oxford and I was left in awe of the dignity and cultivation of all that I encountered. Yes, truly I thought life could be noble and honourable, and scholarship held so many delights.)

Inextricably linked in my mind became the ideas that life was a journey, that man was perfectible, that God desired it so and would help along the way and most strongly of all reading inexhaustibly would lead to the fulfilment of life.

12
Conflicts with John and Helen
"A bedbug would wake her walking past on the pillow."

For both these journeys to the church and to the library, Helen and John still had to take me, even now I was seven, but at this magical age I could choose and take home my own books, (and probably read them by torchlight in bed before two days had passed).

The pain and aggravation I caused my poor sister Helen by my surreptitious reading is too great to recount and I think Helen must have felt she was being subject to one of the punishments of Hades! It never occurred to me that Helen, then and always, was an extraordinarily light sleeper and even with my surreptitious efforts under the blankets the smallest rustle would wake her!

I was so greedy to read that when John had asthma and gave me his tickets to choose books for him, I unashamedly chose books I knew I would like myself! What a row when I returned to my equally, literary-voracious brother and handed him the blatantly, "girly" books, one of which was called "Helen's Babies."! Poor John, how could I have been so cruel? He had already delighted me in bringing home a beautifully illustrated and colourful Parnassus' Treasury of English literature, full of lovely poems and stories, and he let me have that for myself. He had scavenged it from the ruins of Spon Gate school that had been hit by a bomb in the blitz. I remember it chiefly as the first serious book I had ever read that had coloured pictures but also because amid its anthology of poems and extracts, I read the ballad about the little boy who, confined to a wheelchair despaired that he could ever do anything meaningful in his life. To all his complaints, and acting as a refrain to finish each verse, came his patient mother's consoling words,

God has a plan for every man,
And He has one for you!

Of course, the mother's words dramatically were verified. One evening the little boy sat in his wheelchair looking out of the window and unable to sleep. In the darkness of night, he saw the enemies of their town approaching the city walls and gate! Immediately he alerted his parents, who notified the town mayor. The home army were summoned, and the enemy fought off! The little boy who despaired of his purpose in life had saved the city! God had indeed had a plan for him!

What a beautiful inspiring ballad! Of course I knew in my heart that it was a kind of cautionary Victorian tale and couldn't possibly be true, but at the same time a deep conviction settled in my soul that God indeed wanted something from me – from us all, but what possibly could it be?

Yes, this great kindness of John's in giving me that precious book, I had repaid by not even bringing home some suitable library book for him! I was ashamed, but John in his way repaid me by strictly excluding me from sharing in the reading of his precious boys' comic books. It probably wasn't personal because if they became free-for-all in our house, they would not have lasted five minutes! Decades later after John died, his wife Anne told me, with affectionate amusement, how throughout his life he had maintained that same careful habit of storing favourite magazines and refusing to allow them to be shared indiscriminately. Despite John's embargo, in my passion for reading, for several years I would sneak into the front room where my parents let him stash all his boy's comics in the small wardrobe and I would read them secretly when he was out – but he would never let me read them freely. He guarded them like treasure. In those days comics were not the cartoon and picture-dominated booklets they were very soon to become. (It was the American soldiers that first introduced us to the glossy, gaudy picture comics devoted to superheroes.) The traditional boys' comics in England at that time were like a series of short stories and John's comics were called by the flashy names of "The Wizard", "The Hotspur", "The Rover" and "The Adventurer". I read them from cover to cover but the ones I particularly remember were the tales of some boy or youth who started off in life with many obstacles in his path, but who always had burning ambitions and fought desperately, against every opposition to achieve them. There was "Smith of the Lower Third" who won a scholarship and struggled in his private boarding school against all the wealthy classmates, who sensed immediately the limitations of a slum-like upbringing. This probably helped me psychologically to cope with the culture shock of being almost alone in my neighbourhood to pass the grammar school scholarship and don the prestigious (and expensive) Barr's Hill school uniform. The shock too of being part of a minute and conspicuous minority of Catholic or Irish pupils.

There was also, in John's comics, stories of "Tupper of the Track", a youth, recently left school, with a menial job in the gasworks, whose goal was to be a top runner, and who would arrive at competitions, still covered with the grime of work, and would swallow down the remnants of his fish and chip lunch, before leaping into the race and winning, even in spite of the holes in his pumps! There were many, many more such tales of endurance and perseverance and I drank them down like a cat with cream! I never ever queried that no female, regardless of role ever appeared in these stories.

Much, much later I began to wonder how John came to have the privilege of not one but four comics a week, so that he could amass this treasure trove of reading, kept so carefully in the private front room where my parents slept at night. None of the rest of us were bought a single comic, and I'm not surprised because money was so tight. Why then the profligacy with John? It wasn't as if he was a good boy; he was often in trouble. John himself recalled how my mother herself was summoned to Saint Osburg's school to explain why her son invariably arrived at school with dirty hands. It was only when she herself took him for the interview that she discovered that his style of walking to school was by way of dragging his hands firmly along every wall! My main conclusion was that, regardless of naughtiness, perhaps my mother, in that immensely wise and compassionate way she had, realised how desperately John needed to read, especially in the long nights when he could not sleep with his asthma and therefore treated him to an indulgence that the rest of us didn't need. Perhaps also she recognised he had a keen intelligence that no one at school ever acknowledged. I remember the sudden and murderous anger I once felt when I heard a teacher remark that John O' Brien was very good at colouring in! I wanted to hit her.

Certainly, the frequent episodes of John's asthma were some of the most painful memories of my childhood and still bring tears to my eyes as I write. The only relief for asthma in those days was some quack remedy called "Potter's asthma cure". When John had a bad attack, (I don't think I remember one that wasn't bad.), he would sit by the kitchen table, open the little yellow tin box and pour some of the dusty, yellow powder contained within, onto the lid of the box and then after shaping it with matches into a miniature volcano, would light the powder and then try to breathe in the acrid smoke that bellowed out. John's poor head would descend closer and closer to the foul-smelling fumes, trying desperately to breathe it in and relieve his poor lungs. Sometimes, sensing his failure he would jump up in despair and throw open the kitchen door to feel that there was air outside. To know that air existed even though he couldn't breathe it in. I knew him to do this on even the bitterest cold night, as if the pain of his breathing made him oblivious to the pain of cold outside. Often when we went to bed he would remain sitting upright in a chair by the dwindling fire, and how sad to greet that forlorn shape slumped there, when we rose in the morning to get ready for school.

And what of us as we watched? Maybe some of us

would be in tears too, maybe some just drawing or playing very quietly. Maybe my dad and mum would be doing the chores, but all of us inside praying that God would give poor John some respite from that dreadful cross that inflicted him.

What God did give him though was the huge resilience and courage, and good humour and naughtiness too, to put his illness totally away as soon as he felt better! It was as if he compensated for the vacancy of his time of indisposition by throwing himself 150% into whatever else he did. In his final illness, at the age of seventy-four, predictably with bronchial asthma, the doctor deciding to put him into a coma remarked, "This man has not even a sixth of his lung capacity. It's a miracle he could have lived such an active full life till now!" But that was John, he seemed to bubble over with life and energy and despite illness, I would still get a clout from him, if he caught me reading his precious comics! But I never stopped!

Such was my passion for reading. It caused long feuds with Helen too as we shared a bed and I had strict instructions not to keep her awake. Helen slept so lightly that a bedbug might wake her by walking past! My enterprise had to be brilliant then! Torches were my best ally under the covers, but she could hear the rustle of a page turning! Candles! Wait until she went to sleep and then relight the bedtime candle! A wonderful solution until the night my dad went down the garden to put the hens away and saw a little light glowing in our bedroom window. It was next morning when he told us he had gone to our room to find me fast asleep and the candle burnt down to the level of the chair on which I had set it. Candles were never allowed again without supervision. "I told you!" said Helen.

If I was told off about it by my parents I can't remember – rather I think they looked upon it as a miraculous escape and I received some added kindnesses because I hadn't gone up in flames. I was still very precious to them or perhaps they thought I had learned my lesson! John and Helen though weren't so easily swayed to have a good opinion of me. I still stole John's comics and I still disturbed poor Helen with my page-turning in the night.

13

Household Routines

An Hour's Queue for Half a Pound of Sausages

It is extremely hard to convey the multiplicity and variety of all the routines and happenings in a small home crammed full of seven small children. That house moreover was in the city of Coventry, derelict from bombing, and deprived of many of the necessities of life. Fuel was in such short supply that John, Helen, and I would often be sent to the coke yard to buy a quarter of a hundred weight of coke which we would wheel back home on some old pram chassis, to supplement the sparse coal ration. This, as I mentioned, was delivered by big, blackened coal men who carried through to the kitchen big, black, hundredweight bags of coal on their shoulders, to be stored in the coalhouse, hidden behind the table where we ate and occupying the space under the stairs. There were serious shortages in food too, unless you had a lot of money and could buy things on the black market. Food was to remain on rations until 1948 – the year I passed my scholarship to Barr's Hill grammar school, when I was ten. Even after that it was several years before exotic fruits like oranges and bananas became available. (The government though, supplemented our diet, and certainly preserved our good health by issuing free concentrated orange juice and rose hip syrup, and also more repugnantly, thick cod liver oil, which we received by the teaspoonful every morning after breakfast).

I remember well the details of rationing because routinely Helen and I accompanied our mother to a local co-op shop on Spon Street, where we trotted out our Divi number, before the intriguing business of producing all the ration books and cutting out the relevant coupons, for each item of food. (This divi number (short for dividend), recorded the money spent by each customer at the Co-op and at certain times you were rewarded with a small sum of money from a share of the profits made by the company, I suppose Boots has a similar, but less disinterested, scheme with their reward cards!)

Helen always starred in this shopping activity, calculating every price, of every item in her head and often correcting the laboured efforts of the poor shop assistant with her worn-out pencil stub. Beware anyone who tried to overcharge my flustered mother when Helen stood at her side! There would be the one egg a week for each person in the family, two ounces of a rather rancid margarine (seldom butter), and the same of sugar, and cheese. The meat ration my mother would cleverly balance so that always there would be sufficient coupons left for "a decent piece of meat to roast for Sundays".

Coming from the country in Ireland my parents placed a high priority on eating well. Meat must be recognisably meat – my mother never would stoop to the purchase of minced meat, because she couldn't vouch for what was in it. The rest of the week were managed with bacon, offal of all kinds, including my favourite ox heart, roasted with stuffing, faggots from a local faggot and peas shop and the occasional half pound of sausages that Helen and I queued for, interminably, in a shop up near Broadgate. If we had the stamina Helen would coax me to stay another hour to join another queue for half a pound of broken biscuits. Joyful was the rare day when, in response to a rumour and thinking we were in heaven, we were sent to the little shop in Spon street to buy steak pies. They were cooked there to a very haphazard timetable – probably when the ingredients became available. I can taste them now! Potatoes, although boiled with gravy with some meals, was also mashed and served with hot milk, boiled with an onion.

Sometimes at bedtime instead of the customary boiled bread and milk we received a little pyramid of potatoes topped with a ball of butter that as it melted, looked like lava flowing down the sides of a miniature volcano. We could also buy chips of course when we could afford to and we children became quite adept at asking the fish-shop man for "free scratchings" – these were the little scraps of batter that fell from the battered fish bought by more wealthy patrons.

Food then, produced a necessary routine just to stay

alive and healthy. We all endured the routine of swallowing our diluted orange juice and horrible cod liver oil. Dad had the routine of planting his potatoes, cabbage, carrots and onions and of looking after the chickens, who gave an extra valuable few eggs and could be relied on to provide the festive broiler. Sometimes, but this was probably long after the war was over dad would go down to the old market and come back if he were lucky with a couple of herring or perhaps a mackerel. Whenever he made a purchase, he would return with eyes shining and lay out his trophy for all to see. He would stand back and admire the contents of the kitchen table – as proud as if he had caught the fish himself.

Mum, of course, was responsible for the routines of cooking to eke out all the provisions fairly. Bread was eaten in abundance – as a great treat in a jam sandwich, or more often, one made with condensed milk from a tin – or even, strangely, a sugar sandwich, with just a sprinkle of sugar between the slices of bread. Mum also made her huge soda bread cakes favoured with a handful of raisins or a couple of spoonful of black treacle.

In every other aspect of life too I remember a great deal of order and routine. In retrospect this seems quite extraordinary in a house with only four rooms, without a bathroom or hot water and with a toilet sequestered down a path in the garden. As I've said it also lacked electricity and was lit by gas-mantles downstairs and candles in the bedrooms. The day started with us children standing round the kitchen table to eat our porridge and drink our tea. Sunday was the exception when after fasting overnight for Holy Communion we received our rationed egg! Such bliss – even more so if mum had managed to save a little rasher of bacon to fry the egg in! I loved the tea. Dad was usually the chief tea-maker. A proper brew was a handful of Brook Bond or Horniman's tea leaves thrown in a pot already warmed and left to brew at the hob by the fire. Each cup was filled to the brim. Years later I was often mortified when I had made my own effort and poured tea for the family, to hear the scathing comment from my dad, "What's this? Cat's piss" (when I hadn't left it to brew for long) or, "What's this? Half a cup?" (when my judgement fell marginally short of the mind-boggling accuracy and equilibrium needed if the tea were not to gush over the table!) While this was going on mum rekindled the kitchen fire and each in turn had faces wiped by a flannel and Helen and I stood to have hair combed and later plaited. The boys regardless of age usually were well tonsured by the clever attentions of my dad who had bought a barber's clippers, (and saved the family a fortune!) Off then to the routine of school past the bombed craters of Windsor street where occasional standing gables revealed almost indecently, the different choices of bedroom wallpaper; pink roses blooming amidst smashed and broken masonry in some strange, alien environment.

On Barras lane we passed a row of very high and

stately houses elevated by construction high above the pavement. As with my intuitions of people in cars, I imagined these residents to be people of great learning, dignity, and refinement; people whom I would never be able to emulate. Again, I was comforted to think that there was the reality of perfectibility, and that we all could improve. Or perhaps more realistically was I experiencing that syndrome common to immigrants, that in some deep sense they felt themselves inferior to their hosts and could never hope for true equality?

After school, routines were more pronounced! For me the initial routine of going to collect the bread, three big loaves, four and a half pence each (for years and years! No inflation in those days!) I had that task from seven or eight until I was fifteen and moved to Tile Hill. I traversed across a bombed site at the top of Vincent street where the two houses had been hit in the bombing and mostly demolished), down a scary entry, past mounds of ash and refuse left by families who had no dustbins, (or perhaps had been left stranded with no refuse collection in the chaotic days after the Blitz), from there into Thomas Street and then up to the bread shop of dear Mrs Keen, the lady who had met me first when I was two and a half, and fresh from Kiltimagh.

John, I felt, unfairly accused me of bringing scarlet fever into the house when I was five because I played on these ash heaps at the entrance to Thomas Street. I protested strongly and cried, but in my heart I knew that I had been fascinated by the contours and mounds of this miniature moon landscape, with ash hardened into crustaceans by the sun and how often on my errand for the bread I had played leaping from peak to peak! I loved my errand and I loved Mrs Keen, with whom I shared a guilty secret. With the change from the bread (four and a half pence a loaf), I often treated myself to a penny's worth of Mint Imperials. They are to this very day my favourite sweet! I ate them all on my own and I knew Mrs Keen knew of my deception because this was a time when even one sweet could not be purchased without a ration coupon. I suffered greatly from guilt but seemed captivated by my indulgence. And, it puzzles me that I could eat them secretly. Our home consumption of sweets was often restricted to one a day. It also puzzles me that my mum didn't spot the missing penny in the change. But my conscience knew and after I made my First Confession it became my main deliberate sin, along with "I quarrelled with my brothers and sisters". (This latter sin was really a bit of window-dressing because on the whole at this time I was a very timid child and more likely to cry than to fight). Maybe that sin was thrown in for good measure because I was probably the most peaceable child in the family. And maybe it assuaged the guilt of confessing to a sin I knew in my heart I had no intention of correcting!

Have I broken the seal of confession in divulging all

this? God forgive me!

*

Back to routines! Evening and bedtimes. From earliest days John, Helen and I were called "The Big Ones". This was in opposition to the three boys who followed us, Michael, Thomas and James, (or Micky, Tommy and Jimmy) who officially were labelled "The Boys".

And as the family grew in size, the next three children, Teresa, Martin and Edward were called "The Little Ones" – and then, but beyond the parameters of my main story, the last three, arriving most surprisingly when mother was past forty, were known for many years as "The Babies"! These of course were Margaret, Andrew and Francis. They arrived to coincide with the hardest school years of my life, with GCE examinations and "A" and Scholarship exams. Co-incidentally the years of their arrival were the years when academically and unexpectedly, I succeeded beyond anyone's expectation. By the time these three babies, the prettiest children you can imagine, were all established into school, we three "Big Ones" had all of us, left home and married.

Evening routines were dominated by these categories. Although one by one we had to succumb to the evening washing rituals, and although all, even tiny ones participated in some way in prayers usually the rosary), bedtimes were staggered. I remember for many years taking the boys to bed and telling them stories. In this I was copying my dad who had been the storyteller and poem reciter for us big ones, when we were little. I can never remember the stories I told the boys, (they slept, remember, all together in the big double bed with the brass balls on the bedposts) but I do remember clearly that most of the stories I made up afresh each night, and how entranced I was by the gaze of utter love and devotion on those three little faces.

Reflecting on the experience later I queried in my mind how, in choosing a lover, I could ever hope to find the perfection of adoration these children blessed me with. But it wasn't all serious and prim. When I started grammar school and began to learn French, I treated them to all the latest little French songs I learned. My greatest success was with "Sur le Pont D'Avignon", when I acted out, the characters who crossed that bridge at Avignon – especially the drunk man! How they laughed to see my antics! I shared with them also some of the ballads my father had told us and some I was learning myself at school. We, all of us, remembered, and loved "The Wreck of the Hesperus" by Longfellow and "Lord Ullins Daughter" by Thomas

Campbell. I added numerous others of my favourites that I find I remember to this day.

Whilst the boys were being sent into dreamland, mother would be downstairs feeding or rocking the little ones. Dad himself, if home from work loved to rock the baby in his arms, often with his toe tapping up and down as if he were playing his tin whistle. By the time I re-joined them downstairs it was time for us privileged ones to sit by the fire for an hour or so to read or play quietly. The most wonderful thing about this time was that we could watch the activities of our parents. Dad might be mending the boys' boots with his cobbler's last (a heavy three-pronged tool with prongs to shape the shoes) and real thick yellow leather, which he soaked to make pliable. What a fortune he must have saved, and we would watch as he finished off the job by hammering metal studs into the toecaps and the heels of the boys' boots, the parts which took the greatest strain. At Christmas time he would be busy carving little wooden toys for the boys' presents. The most impressive of these was a wooden horse big enough for James to sit on at the age of two – or push when he could walk properly, as he was still unsteady on his feet. He carved little cars and lorries and one ingenious one had a driver sitting at the front of the van wearing a flat cap. Father showed us how you could put a penny on the cap and then the little driver would tip backwards and the penny would slide into an aperture in the roof of the van. Revealing it to be a money box as well as a toy truck!

My mother too would be busy with sewing and mending and making her rag rugs, cutting strips of material from discarded clothing. She would place them when finished by our bedsides to warm our feet against the cold linoleum which covered most of the floors in the house. She could crochet too and made berets for me and Helen – but I never saw her attempt anything more complicated, except perhaps little blankets for the babies. This could have been more a matter of shortage of wool though rather than lack of skill, because this was an era when fair isle knitting came into vogue, fashioned as it was by multiple and very beautiful patterns made of many colours. It didn't need a whole ball of wool but instead lots of shorter strands, often those unwound from a previous garment.

On special occasions visitors came – usually fellow immigrants from Mayo, and some even from Kiltimagh. We were quiet and listened to the talk, never interrupting until the nod was given to disappear to bed. Occasionally they might notice us and involve us in some interchange and I especially remember a small old man, James Carney who talked always, without pause or inflection who asked me unexpectedly what was the definition of a bomb. I was mortified to confess my ignorance of such a profound piece of knowledge! He narrated the definition to me advising me to learn it well by heart. "A bomb is an elongated, symmetrical, miniature, compound projectile," he advised me, with the instruction to learn that definition firmly by heart. I did as he advised and was most proud of my new impressive knowledge, not stopping to query why he didn't mention the most important quality of all, the bomb's capacity to kill and maim thousands of fellow human beings. How engrossed they were in their talk and how nervous my poor mother got when talk strayed to the "Troubles" and the dangers of the IRA. She would say, "Don't be talking now of such things, anyone could be listening outside the door." and my dad would laugh at her and say "Isn't it our own house we're in and don't I work hard enough to pay the rent!"

Now years later I marvel to remember the order and routine of those early childhood days. No longer disturbed by sirens and trips to the shelter, for the most part bright and healthy, (apart from John's struggles with the asthma), we children grew and thrived in a security that seemed blessed. Indeed, I'm sure it was.

14
Up The Top
"Children Rule – OKAY?"

If I were to consider my childhood life as a triangle, (ridiculous idea I know, but I struggle to convey how all the different areas of my life intermeshed). But if as I said, my life were a triangle, family life and routines would be one side, school and church would be another and the third, probably the hypotenuse, if it were a right-angled triangle would definitely be, "Up The Top"!

Have I mentioned this phrase before? It was used by us all, adults as well as children, to denote the bleak spread of land that had been left by the bombing of two, possibly four terraced houses at the end of Vincent street, and the land too that had once been their gardens. After the worst of the rubble had been cleared away the waste land spread across to the abandoned back gardens of nearby Thomas street, down to the then unguarded and dangerous, muddy banks of the river Sherbourne. To the right there was open access to Vincent Street itself where on the other side of the road the terrace was neatly completed, unscathed by bombing. On our side of the street, (the even numbers), the families were all Irish and Catholic with plentiful children. On the other side, (the odd numbers) there were older, more staid residents, (Coventrians and Protestant, we thought), with only one child I remember in the whole of their side of the street. There were several dogs, including two particularly ugly Pekinese dogs that frightened me.

The Protestants had an intense dislike for us children, bordering on contempt as evidenced by some of the men trying to bribe us with pennies if we would clean the dog poo from their gardens. For a time, the two sides of the street were separated by old, cement square bomb shelters, those rarely used even in the most dangerous raids, because of the appalling smell of urine. Once the shelters were demolished the enmity and separation became even more intense. Looking back, I am not at all surprised this should be so, for those many Irish children lived their lives out-of-doors and in the most exuberant ways imaginable. They also seemed to attract every sparky child from the streets around. For elderly, staid, conventional Coventrians the noise and activity of all those children must have come as a torture more devastating than the Blitz!

That wide spread of land at the top of Vincent street, we called "Up The Top"! What a magical life was lived there! Who wanted to stay in their house when you could go out to play, "Up The Top"! All the children wanted the same thing after school – to go out to play! Age hardly came into it – from five to fourteen-year olds, all came out to play. Sex didn't come into it either, whether boy or girl, activities encompassed both genders, though there still remained some few divisions by inclination, like the ball games and skipping for girls, and the marbles, cigarette cards and conker-bashing for boys.

Money didn't come into it either. The few balls available were often made from the rubber rings cut from discarded, bicycle inner-tubes – they bounced very well but just a little wonky. Bikes we had never seen because in those days no one possessed such a thing as a bike. Old pram chassis were the nearest we ever got to mechanised transport, often embellished with a plywood contraption for a seat and rope looped round the front wheels for steerage. The breaking mechanism was a brave foot inserted on top of one of the speeding wheels – enough to take off the foot itself if left there too long!

Metal, rubber and all associated materials and skills had been diverted for years now to the war effort, so improvisation was the name of the game amongst those children. Bats were carved from wood, as were the little wooden pegs we used to play a game called "tippet". The chassis of old prams were the most sophisticated by far of all the playing aids and were used not only as useful trolleys to fetch coke from the gas yard for our parents, but also for fetching wood and branches and old motor car tyres in the bonfire season, and for mad charioteer races for the big boys, as they scooted down the middle of the street.

I can't begin to describe the richness of all that "Up the Top" activity or the multitude of the children who gathered there as if by a magnet drawn from nearby streets,

Thomas Street, Trafalgar Street, Hope Street and even Upper York Street the location of the bloody and fearful abattoir. (Wherever did those doomed animals come from? I never heard it discussed.) The children gathered as soon as school was over and perhaps the "messages" (chores) done, but also for most free time on Saturday and, glory of glory, most of the long, light-filled days of the six week summer holiday from school.

In our family, and the families of most of the other Catholic children, Sunday was kept as a family day. There was early mass, so that we could go to communion after fasting all night, and the special Sunday lunch of roast meat (lamb, beef or pork), and vegetables, usually cabbage and carrots from the garden. with gravy and sometimes stuffing or Yorkshire pudding. As I mentioned before mam was always very clever and disciplined to save enough coupons for that "decent piece of meat". When it was nearly ready and taken out of the oven to be inspected, we were lucky indeed to have a crust of bread handy to dip into the succulent juices! After lunch on Sunday, came the big family exodus, the family walk. Mum, dad, (with his cap on of course and a newspaper tucked in his jacket pocket, but never "The News of the World"!), the pram too, a big Silver Cross, usually containing two of the babies, and us lot – always clean and dressed in our best and always I remember with a great sense of excitement about our destination. Would it be to Hearsall Common, passing the magical shiny blue roof of Saint Mary Magdalene's church on Hearsall lane. It lightens the heart to this day as you glimpse it through the bus window. Or perhaps we would go to Spenser Park with its view over the railway lines and a chance to dance on the bridge in the smoke bellowing up from the rare steam train? Would we walk much further to the wonderful Park, later we found was called the War Memorial park, where we could see lovely coloured tropical birds and run like crazy across the huge fields there. Maybe we would go, quaking with fear, to the place the boys called "Devils Dungeon" or continue the road on to Crackley woods, bordering on Kenilworth, and pick bluebells, if it was the season. How ruthless we were! Our arms were filled, and the white sap was dripping from the now lifeless stems like streams of tears, mourning our heartless butchery! (Did those flowers ever reach home in the end?) There was Watery Lane too or even, home from home, my beloved Sandpit, at the Butts. How many hours I must have spent, sitting, in the midst of the sand, making my own little world.

But back to the "TOP"! So many friends. So many songs. So many games. So many sun-scorched days that turned our legs bright red, most inappropriate for walking in the May processions at Church on Sunday, in our special, best, white dresses. "Up The Top." We were running and jumping; throwing and catching; hiding and seeking; laughing and crying; watching and copying; and trying,

trying, ever trying to run faster for longer, jump further, catch quicker, throw harder, and even in all the hubbub, select the one to fall in love with – but never breathe a word!

Seasonal activities sometimes dominated with Bonfire night being by far the most exciting. The season for the boys began as early as September with the gathering of wood and anything combustible. The activity was heightened in suspense by the boys forming bonfire gangs each collecting for their own particular fire at Trafalgar Street or Starley Road or York Street or Vincent Street. As each fire grew in size neighbouring gangs consumed with envy would make a raid and flee back to their own base bearing the trophies of huge branches, old floorboards or the seemingly ubiquitous used car tyres. Such an insult could not be ignored and within days a return onslaught would be made. Imagine the permutations of revenge visits as the four main contestants vied for supremacy! For months this continued – until that happy day on November 5th, when Bonfire night finally arrived. When all honours were considered satisfied and with fireworks bought by the parents, entire families came out of their houses to behold the magnificence of that fire, with the silly little effigy of a man tied to the topmost stake and was that Mister Skalley's cap fixed on his head? It never occurred to us, then, that the villain we were burning was indeed a Catholic like ourselves, but as with the IRA, no Catholic there would have had any sympathy for the violence of his methods. No it was just a game, a glorious, exciting, rule-breaking, dangerous, magical game!

There was daylight in the night-time, children out of their beds, mothers and fathers revelling like children, and everywhere the bang and whistle and whoosh and sparkle of fireworks being fired from every direction, Jumping jacks jumped around like imps with a mind of their own, making the children run and scream. Catherine wheels whirled sending out circles of glittering stars of every colour, unless sometimes, the wheel was dislodged and the sparks toasted your knickers! And with a roared "Stand back! Stand back!" rockets whooshed into the air aiming for the moon, in days when the moon was still an inaccessible target! As the evening passed and the fire grew less some of the mothers would bring out potatoes to bury in the embers. If we were lucky, we would receive a blackened spud, delicious when the crumbling skin was discarded.

In the morning before school we would look to see some faint glowing debris left at the heart of the fire, and everywhere the abandoned cases of the rockets or Catherine wheels or bangers. The air itself would be thick and murky and the acrid smell of gunpowder made your nostrils smart. We were happy though. It was as if we had experienced a catharsis. Did we just forget all about big Pat Dowd, still in hospital months later, with a leg so badly scorched by the burning car tyre someone had thrown at him, from which he couldn't extricate himself? And our John himself, still wearing the bandages on his wrist from an injury caused by holding a lit firework too long and now necessitating a painful half hour of dressing before school by my mum, every day for weeks after. We loved the bonfires so much. The accidents just seemed a necessary evil. Bonfire night remained in our memory as a time of great joy and excitement and most precious of all, of the closest communion, all the kids together, all the mums and dads, and not a copper to be seen anywhere!

Such was life in up the Top. Too, too much to write about. Too, too many children to write about. An intricate, teeming, warren of activity and endeavour. The second home of our childhood. We were surely blessed.

15

Back to Education
"Not Fat Henry VIII Again!"

I return now from describing that hypotenuse of my life, "UP THE TOP" where we went sliding down in thoughtless pleasure, just as we did down the shelter roofs of Grey friar's Green where I ripped my best silk bloomers – I return, I say, to a part of life that was no longer the sides of a triangle but more like the area of the triangle itself. This is not to say that all the other aspects of life ceased to exist but that something was changing and emerging and was soon to dominate my inner life. It was also to have a profound influence on the rest of my life and would alter completely my experience and identity of being a "Catholic, Irish, Immigrant child".

At that time in Coventry, in 1946, most children attended what we called "all-age" schools. You started school at five years of age and left when you were fourteen years; the boys to start wearing long trousers and looking for a job, the girls to have their plaits cut off and begin to think of looking for a man. Maybe during the last few years of your schooling, you missed a few weeks each year at harvest time as you were taken to nearby farms to help with potato-picking. Not enough soldiers had returned yet to enable men to do the job and potatoes were an indispensable part of the nation's diet. Each class in the school, at whatever level, had its own teacher who taught all subjects. This meant of necessity that many subjects were given the briefest of attentions. Teachers then had qualified in their profession after a two years course in a teacher's training college – and after the war an increasing number gained their expertise in the wartime emergency training scheme lasting one year. I don't ever remember professional development being entertained as a concept. But how would I know, anyway?

    Classes were large usually between fifty five and sixty pupils, and this was especially true of the Catholic schools in Coventry because of the huge influx of Irish immigrants arriving to work in the munitions and later car industries, and then, when the war was over, and the blitz had blitzed, there was work-a-plenty in rebuilding the city. It must be remembered though, that the Irish came in hope, in response to the adverts for labour posted in remote areas of Ireland, like Mayo, by the British government. Mayo itself with its rocky land and poor agricultural yield was fertile ground for recruitment. Of course, my father himself was one of the very many young men who came to England knowing full well he could never support his growing family in Ireland from the frugal fruits of their few acres. Even today in 2017, small peasant farmers can only survive there with the aid of generous grants from the E.U. As I've been reminded by my two cousins on my father's side still living there.

Education then was rudimentary in its scope and content. English, (reading and writing), arithmetic and religious knowledge took a disproportionate amount of time and the strongest focus in each of these subjects was on learning by rote. In English it was spelling and wonderful, wonderful, indispensable, heavenly!!! – Poetry! Arithmetic of course was fixated on tables (so many more then in the days before the conversion to the metric system. The old pound with twelve pennies to a shilling and twenty shillings to a pound implied a fluency with the twelve times tables. The old weighing system meant you needed to calculate in fourteens and sixteens, because there were sixteen ounces in a pound and fourteen pounds in a stone. And now I can boast "See how clearly I had those facts engraved upon my brain that more than seventy years later they are still second nature!")

In R.E. the emphasis was on learning the penny catechism by heart. We would also spend time in learning the Latin responses in the mass and their meaning. It was to be decades before the mass was finally changed to the vernacular and we fully understood the liturgy. But – how lovely and special it sounded, and how it captured the awe and sanctity of the service. Maybe it did that most important thing of all, by convincing one of the existence of another superior reality that beckoned one to aspire to nebulous virtues and loves beyond the reach of man. As the poet Browning wrote, "A man's reach must exceed his grasp or what's a heaven for?". Or as Viktor Frankl concluded in his wise and moving book, "Man's Search for Meaning,"

"Self-actualisation can only be achieved by self-transcendence." I knew it then but I couldn't put it into words. The mass began,

> *Sacredos (Priest) "Introibo ad altare Dei..".*
> *Minister (Server). "Ad Deum qui laetificat juventutem meam"*
> *"I will go unto the altar of God, to God who gives joy to my youth".*

What a lovely thought. That there is a God: that we can approach him closely and we young ones are especially lucky because he gives us great joy – and joy is so much more than happiness.

My best friend Pauline Croker (I remind you again of this little friend that so often galvanised me in intellectual pursuits and more dangerously, physical challenges) this friend and I set ourselves the task of learning all the responses of the mass by heart so that we could make a case to become girl servers on the altar. Serving mass was at that time an activity strictly reserved for males and we had watched with envy the boys in their long white albs looking like the young angels in Renaissance paintings as they helped the priest in the various activities of the ritual. They also joined in the many Latin responses and prayers that punctuated the service.

Pauline and I thought if we could learn all the main prayers of the mass by heart, we could also join this special male elite on the altar. We included in our repertoire the long Latin prayers of the Confiteor, the Gloria, and the Credo. There was also the Sanctus, the Pater Noster and the Agnus Dei. Alas! In spite of our prowess we were to convince no one of our belief in the equality of the sexes at eight years of age and it was to be many, many years before the Church changed its ruling on this same matter. Now as I watch some of the little girls I taught in Catechesis serving the priest at mass, with grace and reverence I wonder sadly why it took so long for the Church to recognise this source of strength and richness in its midst. And little girls were deprived of this loving and grace-filled experience.

I see now that in each of the subjects, I mentioned (referred to in common parlance as the three "Rs") learning by heart could have considerable practical advantages in effecting a huge saving in money spent on books and paper, both in very short supply after the war, and also would have spared overworked teachers a lot of the marking drudgery necessitated in correcting the work of sixty pupils. It puzzled me exceedingly at that time that these three subjects could be called the three "Rs" when writing began with a "W" and arithmetic with an "A". Perhaps someone in the education department had a sense of humour? Or was it just an ironical mocking of the pronunciation of these poor state scholars?

History as a subject seemed to be an endless retelling of the disastrous events of the English Reformation, with great emphasis on the villainous and lustful and very fat Henry VIII, and most marks seemed to be gained in exams always by an accurate recitation of the names of his six wives – and the details of their demise. Certainly, few other countries were featured in our nationalistic curriculum. Glancing at TV programmes over the last two years it did occur to me recently that the nation was perhaps regressing to some of those fixations of pre-war History. Even my history degree too in the 1950s struck me as disproportionate in its emphasis on the less subtle and less complex reasons there may have been for the Reformation. And why was so much about England? (How happy I had been at Manchester university to have followed a year-long course under the inspiring tutelage of Professor Johns on the Golden Age of Ireland.)

Geography and Science were virtually non-existent as subjects of study. Music veered between lusty renderings of English folk songs that resounded across the playground with echoes akin to John Peel's "Halloo",

Do you ken John Peel, at the break of day
Do you ken John Peel when he's far far away......

I will include the words in my epilogue, alongside our other favourite, "Early One morning, Just as the sun was dawning", I will leave it to you to find the tunes I promise you you will not be disappointed.

In stark contrast to this carefree ebullience was the nightmarish experience, also called music, of being nailed in one's desk to face a sheet of strange symbols to which, by some mysterious process of intuition we were expected to respond with sounds like "Ta.. Ta.. Tate..Ta," and endless variations of the same. The symbols were neither numbers or letters. What could they be?... What could they be? The blows of mystification to an intelligent mind were not as severe in impact as the vicious raps from a cruel knuckle that landed on my skull if a "Ta" was diagnosed as misplaced in the class' mindless cacophony. As the lesson progressed the knuckle raps on my head from the cruelly hovering teacher became more frequent as I disintegrated into a gibbering "ta ta" machine!

I attribute a lot of my later terror of music to this particular form of torture as a child. Not even the nightly playing of my father's lovely flute or the beautiful harmonies of my Church music and all the beautiful hymns could restore in me a conviction that music would ever be within the grasp of my own personal understanding or achievement. Now as I haltingly pick out a tune with one hand on my lovely piano and listen later to my daughter's Bach or the effortless trills of my youngest son's Mozart, I suffer the pain of realising the loss of some potential that was needlessly and cruelly douched. I understand also as a teacher what may have caused some unhappy pupils to become so totally stymied in their academic studies and I curse with unchristian zeal anyone who stunts the hopes of a child in his or her pursuit of learning.

P.E., as I mentioned before could only be described as an anaemic version of military square-bashing, always in straight lines, always in strict silence. The few forays into the athletic skills of racing and high jump were often curtailed abruptly by accidents, as fledgling high jumpers landed awkwardly in the playground, on hard concrete, barely covered with thin coconut matting. My brother Tom, always a promising athlete and sportsman. broke his femur in just such an endeavour and he remembered with mortification all his life how mam had to push him to the hospital in a baby's pram for months after for physiotherapy. You'll be relieved to know though, that in spite of this, in his teenage years he excelled both in running and high jump and represented the new Catholic Comprehensive Ullathorne school with great success! He told me just recently that to fully recover he had set himself a target to run the three miles to Ullathorne, there and back for two years, before he began to excel again.

There were one or two highlights to our educational experience as with the occasion of a visiting actor, in solitary splendour, reciting scenes from Shakespeare to the whole school in the dinner hall; or the time when a team of players came to act out the play of Rumplestiltskin in the playground. To us, this latter seemed so much more magical because the actors all had different costumes and looked so beautiful. In the Shakespeare entertainment there was a dreadful puzzle to work out – which side of the actor's face was the female, and then, when he did an abrupt turnaround which was the man he would become – beard up or beard down!

Altogether though, even at nine years of age when I adored school, there were many reservations in my appreciation of that long, longed-for education. The reservations grew stronger as I grew older. Can you imagine then, at the age of nine, to realise suddenly that it didn't have to be always like this, that if you worked very hard, and had inordinate luck, you could sit some test papers in English, essay writing and arithmetic. You could, by some as yet unknown process, "PASS THE SCHOLARSHIP".

16

The Scholarship
"In Search of the Holy Grail"

Passing the Scholarship was a very momentous event because it meant you could progress to an entirely different form of education. I suppose I learned most about this because Helen was at that age of moving towards eleven and it was known throughout the school what a clever girl she was, who would surely pass. It was well known also, however, that Catholic schools had a dismal record in their success rates. (Maybe the class sizes were too large – sixty was not uncommon coupled with good Catholic teachers being in shorter supply? This would not be surprising when one considers that Catholics only gained access to college education in the 1920s. Maybe some Catholic schools were not long recovered from the blitzing they had received and didn't have adequate resources?) Whatever the reason or reasons, for years at Saint Osburg's it had never been known that more than one child passed the scholarship in the one year. Coventry at that time had very few grammar schools and one technical college for boys. There were no Catholic grammar schools at all.

Shining alongside Helen in her class was an equally gifted girl called Francine Barlowe. An only child, tall and assured, not in the least bit Irish, but prodigiously gifted they said. So this was to be the year when records were to be broken and two children would gain the honour of progressing to the Grammar school! Helen with her computer-like brain and the sharpest critical abilities, and Francine, with her outstanding prowess and with devoted, knowledgeable parents to guide her. (Helen told me after she read this, that there were two other friends of hers who were extremely bright and hard-working who also longed for a grammar school place.)

Helen briefed me intensely about this Grammar school that she hoped to go. You had so many different subjects to study, with lots of different teachers. You could learn another "real" language like French or German as well as the Latin we had encountered at Church. Everywhere was wonderful equipment, like art rooms with paint, science labs with little fires, and dangerous acids, Gymnastic rooms with ropes to climb and parallel bars to balance on, and every kind of ball and hoop and skipping rope, and and ..... everything! You could even, if you had enough money, learn to speak properly by taking lessons, but since this "standard or Oxford English" consisted mainly. it was rumoured, of repeating "How now Brown cow?" Helen personally didn't think it was worth it! This new subject was called Elocution, and it helped you to speak like a proper English person.

When the results of Helen's year arrived after weeks of nail-biting tension, Saint Osburg's school was revealed to have maintained its tradition. Only one child, as usual, had passed. That child was Francine Barlowe! It was at school that the main shock waves were felt and expressed. My parents were philosophical – "well she still has the good brain on her, she'll make something of her life!" was their comment – but the teachers! Such an uproar! Not that they ever denied the justice of Francine Barlowe gaining a Grammar school place, (That she was truly gifted was born out by her achievement in gaining a place years later to read maths at Cambridge, in days when girls were seldom admitted and certainly not from a half-bombed city Grammar school. (In my own time, and as late as the 1950s, it was not even countenanced that the grammar school could submit a candidate to apply for Oxford or Cambridge unless she had studied for an extra year in the sixth-form.) My yearning to go to Oxford originated after I had cycled there at the age of fifteen with a group of friends to be dazzled and enthralled by its beauty and dignity. Even with that motivation though to apply there in my six-form years another year at school I thought, would be a price too high to pay.

But the furore at school from headmaster down, was all about Helen – how could she not pass? That girl was exceptional from the age of five! Appeals were made and battles fought on Helen's behalf until at last she was afforded the rare privilege of taking another exam to gain entrance to a grammar school in Birmingham. But, she didn't pass this exam either. The vision that Helen had painted of the grammar school had been irresistible. I had often walked in Helen's shadow so, I concluded, irresistible or not, if she couldn't pass the scholarship, what chance had I?

I kept my head low in the face of Helen's intense disappointment – a disappointment made worse in many ways by the disappointment of all her teachers. Only mum and dad, without telling anyone started to put a little bit of money by for her, to pay for a three month training course in shorthand and typing at a private secretarial college when she left school at fourteen. (I think I tell a lie here as I suddenly remember how hard up we were then and it was three whole years later that dad and mum after hours of debate, ventured into debt by buying that great luxury, the very first wireless for the family – and this was only enabled by the new payment method of hire-purchase.) I'm sure that that was their intention at the time though, to give Helen this chance, whenever they could. Fortunately by the time she left school they could afford it and Helen broke every record in speed tests and words per minute and left to procure an excellent job as a personal secretary to a big guy in the Tax Office. As for me, I was to carry on with the usual, ("Same as.... same as....") as I hear the young ones say these days. "Same as" – but without the hope.

But then a truly amazing thing happened! A young male teacher was discharged from the army where he had been fighting in Africa and, returning to his hometown of Coventry, was given our class to teach for the whole of the eighteen months preceding the scholarship. At that time in 1946 and 1947, these de-mobbed young men were referred to as the "demob-happy," such was their enthusiasm and optimism. Having survived the horrors of war and intoxicated with the declaration of peace and victory, they arrived into civilian life convinced of their powers to transform the world.

What Guardian angel was at my shoulder to place such a man as my teacher to prepare me for the scholarship? When the bursting need to give and nurture and inspire encounters the bursting need to receive and learn and emulate and please, and this in a world that is suddenly good again and ripe with potential, miracles can happen and the mind can grow and flower like a blossom tree in Spring – like a lovely tree of Japanese cherry blossom. So it was with me at nine years of age. Again the scholarship was within reach.

This teacher, this amazing teacher, was Mr. Lilley. Handsome and strong and still tanned brown from his time wearing those "Boots, boots, boots, marching over Africa!" he burst into our lives to convince us of our amazing intelligence, our capacity to work, our ability to memorise, our speed to respond to whatever demand was made by the lesson or task in hand. (You will dearly love Rudyard Kipling's rousing poem and of course I will include it at the end of my story.) More than anything else he filled us with hope and confidence and a deep conviction that ours was to be the class that broke all the records and little Catholic pupils and little Irish pupils would join at last on a much more equal footing the predominantly Protestant and English students who thronged the City grammar and technical schools. It would no longer be "No Blacks, No Dogs, NO Irish!"

Mr Lilley remained throughout my life at the pinnacle of the recipients of my love, gratitude and admiration. I almost wrote the word "worship" but it came to my mind a sharp reprimand I had once received for describing thus a man of particularly inspirational influence. "Only God can be given worship!" I was chastised. But now I wonder why it should ever go amiss to address and praise in another human being, with awe and admiration, gratitude to find in them some quality akin to that of the Divine? Didn't God after all make us in His image? More important to focus on was that the war had been won, a brave new world was about to emerge, and we, tiny scraps of humanity, mainly from the slum-like conditions of a bombed-out Coventry, would be the breeze to help lift the wings of the Phoenix rising from the ashes of our poor, ruined, but enormously resilient city. We would be educated and help to change the world.

My friend Pauline and I, amidst the hundreds of poems we learned that year, responded in particular to "If" by Rudyard Kipling, first read to us by Mr. Lilley, influenced no doubt by the valour of his "Boots" poem,

If you could force your heart and nerve and sinew
To serve their turn long after they have gone,
And still hold on when there is nothing in them
Except the will that says to them, "Hold on"!

If you can fill the unforgiving minute,
With sixty seconds worth of distance run.
Yours is the earth and everything that's in it,
And what is more you'll be a man my son.

This poem of course will be included in my short anthology of these poems that did so much to form my identity as a "Catholic, Irish immigrant child". What I didn't know then though that this same poem "If" by Rudyard Kipling was nominated by BBC's TV Bookworm programme as the Nations favourite poem. How amazing that a poem could retain such a universal appeal for seventy years! This increasing devotion to poetry, though was beginning to loosen the bonds that bound me so tightly to many aspects of my Irish culture and was introducing into a greedy heart, a longing and desire for strange and unknown realms of knowledge that would lead me far away from the "me" I was then, to a distant "me" whom I believed, was more the me, who would not be "me" if that first "me" were to go.

Conundrums indeed!

17

Interim

"What a Feckin' Winter!"

How swiftly those eighteen months passed until the date of the Scholarship. At the end of 1946, the most joyous of Christmases, with dad's paper chains and colourful tissue bells and balls adorning the kitchen, the big, fat chicken from the garden, strangled and made into dad's famous broth. Presents were prepared, small but exciting. Some for the boys made by my dad, many coming from Saint Joseph's convent in Kenilworth to which Helen and I had trecked the long road to collect from the nuns. The presents for the poor (or poorer!) children. There were lollipops too from an American "Care" parcel sent by Uncle John and Aunt Alice in Philadelphia, and of course most of all we looked forward to the lovely mass at Saint Osburg's with the nativity crib and the big shining star above it. Baby Jesus was going to be born! Carols were sung and scruffy little carol singers came to our door. We were not yet old enough to be allowed to go on our own to join in the singing.

    The biggest present of all, to the family, arrived on December 27th, 1946 with the nativity of baby Martin. (If you think this phrase disrespectful isn't that what every birth is, the coming of a perfect one, a complete and special innocent, a fresh chance yet again to mend our broken world?) Teresa now was two years old and a bonny, placid, smiling girl with bright auburn curls. Martin was equally robust and seemed destined for a trouble-free childhood. It didn't quite happen like that though for within days of his birth, there struck without warning, the severest winter within living memory. Our first recognition of this was to find, as we clamoured as usual to go to the outside lavatory in the morning, no one could open the door. Also there percolated through the drawn curtains an eerie light. Looking out we found the back door was blocked by a five-foot drift of snow and everything around was white. It took a good hour for my dad to descend from an upstairs window to manhandle the worst of the snow from the door jamb and give respite to some aching bladders.

For the next four months we led a snow-bound existence. Such great hardship as we struggled to keep warm and clean (how could you wash clothes often when there was no way of drying them) We struggled to get fuel for the fire, so John, Helen and I were sent interminably to the coke yard with the pram chassis to plead for a quarter-hundred of knobbly coke to add some heat to the ration of coal. We struggled too to get enough nourishing food, so we hung about the faggot and peas shop to get first in the queue if they should chance to open. Struggling likewise to sleep in icy bedrooms unless dad relented to our grumbles and brought up a shovelful of burning coals to put in the miniature bedroom grate. Beneath the picture of Jesus walking on the waters. Maybe it was a blessing to have so many people together and at least share some body warmth.

Sometimes the whole family seemed to gather close together around the kitchen fire, (shielded as it was with drying nappies, it was still the warmest place in the house) and I remember one day when I missed my chance to squeeze into one of the tiny little stools next to the grate and found myself forlornly facing a wall of backs, whose owners were obviously basking in the desirable warmth. I decided I couldn't compete and finding my coat, opened the back door and walked out into the deep snow and kept on walking until it began to get dark. Scott himself couldn't have equalled the nobility of that gesture.! To my surprise I found I was feeling warm and with an extraordinary peace in my heart. I realised that for the first time in my life I had done something that was unselfish. I had let the others enjoy the fire and not drawn attention to myself.

You can imagine how the winter passed. There were snowballs and snow fights and snowmen and our very own invention – a snow maze. After the collaborative and painstaking work of all the children, the whole of "Up the Top" was covered with walls of snow, intricately weaving together to make walkways with the occasional dead-end. These walls were about two feet high and quite thick, so you can imagine how much snow must have fallen to have built such a structure. Another fascinating occupation was introduced by the members of a wild Dublin family, who arrived in nearby Thomas Street, reputed to be twenty in number, and who shocked us to the core with their plentiful use of the swear word "feckin". We had our own hierarchy of forbidden words of course. How we knew them God only knows because they were rarely spoken even by the most reprobate and certainly never by my parents. (My father however did have his Irish terms of abuse referring to "omathauns" or "lachecos". "Damn" and "blast" were on the lowest level of our children's hierarchy. Above, of a more serious nature, we placed "bloody" and "bugger". At the pinnacle of evil was the "f" word and "bastard", probably nearing mortal sin status. None of these words were used by us but these Dublin kids couldn't finish a sentence without using the word perilously close to our "F" word. You can guess the word was "feckin'". We didn't tell on these children at home because they also had great ideas, and we would have been stopped from playing with them. I did though notice a strange look from my mum when we mentioned the word "Dubliners." Could it be then, I wondered, that there was a group in Ireland reviled even more than the "Kiltchies" like us?? One wonderful invention of theirs was to make the longest and fastest slide in the world. Now thinking about it, it seems a miracle that every mother in Vincent Street didn't end up with a broken leg. Down the entire street pavement, from top to bottom, we cleared away all loose snow and then brought buckets of water to slowly slosh along its length ......slowly, slowly, giving it a chance to freeze as it fell. The result was a long sheet of ice that would have graced any public rink,if they had had them in those days. The top of the slide near the lamp post was left with powdery snow to provide sufficient run-up space. So, you took a good run, worked up a good speed and hurtled yourself, with arms outstretched for balance, on to the glistening surface. We small ones only attempted to join the slide in places and wobbled along. The big boys though flew down at the speed of light and for a final burst of speed at the end "went down on their hunkers". I have never forgotten this beautiful word that those wild Dubliners introduced us to – the word that means to sit down on your haunches, or ankles. "Hunkers"!

I have been a bit ashamed to mention so far that this disgraceful family from Dublin that "fecked" their way through every conversation, had the same surname as our own family. They were too numerous to count, (even more so than us) and they too were called O'Brien. Now though, we lost our shame, briefly – the slide was so glorious we christened it after the inventors, the "O'Brien slide". And although we would have punched anyone who suggested that we were relatives of these alien creatures from Strumpet city, we allowed them this moment of glory.

Winter passed though, green shoots appeared in the ground and baby Martin grew fat and strong. All this time at school Mr Lilley had surmounted the rival appeals of snow and slides and kept our minds firmly fixed on the goal that lay ahead, the preparations for the scholarship, every day beginning with mental arithmetic. We wrote stories galore and every spare moment demanded a "silent reader" for company. Many weeks we memorised two or even three poems and took turns in reciting them to the class. Don't ask me about mathematics – we were introduced to things we had never before encountered, and probably never would again – the calculation of compound interest for instance, which sums covered several pages, or the best way to read a gas meter and the reasons behind it! But how he, this demob-happy Mr Lilley, talked and talked and questioned and cajoled and seemed to pour from his strong, young body like a blood transfusion for us pupils, the energy and spirit that we were going to need in our great enterprise. To pass the Scholarship.

The months passed on and finally in the early summer the great day came, and we took our scholarship. To use a corny phrase, we met our Waterloo. Considering all the anticipation and its great importance I recall remarkably little about it. At least I didn't make a huge blot, manipulating those peculiar pens that you dipped in the inkwell in your desk. That had always been a weakness of mine. I just sat there and did what was asked of me, without emotion. Perhaps I was saving the emotion for all that would transpire when we were given our results.

I was certainly to need it.

18

Waiting……. Waiting…
"Like Flies on the Flank of a Whale"

We had two months yet to wait for the scholarship results and in this interim time just two major memories emerge in my mind as worthy of sharing. What was their significance you must decide for yourself? The first tells you something about the extraordinary latitude granted to children in those days, and also about the pride in my character that could be foolhardy to the point of death. The second memory though is the reverse of pride but reveals alongside deep insecurity, the depth of my longing to progress in my education.

I alluded earlier in my story to the many ambitious enterprises undertaken by me and my best friend Pauline Croker. Alongside the intellectual, I said some of these were physical, and maybe dangerous. Looking back, that now seems to be an understatement. I should substitute for "dangerous" the word "deadly". One summer evening, accompanying our older sisters, Helen and Margaret Croker to their Children of Mary prayer group at Saint Osburg's Church, Pauline and I, considered by the teacher too young for prolonged praying, found ourselves whiling the time away in the deserted school playground next to the church. We were fascinated to notice that continuing repairs to the roof of the school, not yet completed after the war damage, necessitated new scaffolding that led all the way from a balcony to the apex of the roof itself.

No harm in climbing to the balcony. Once there, a further ladder beckoned irresistibly. And now, oh scary excitement, we had access to the school roof itself. Thirty feet above the school yard, it was covered we found, with a sort of green tarpaulin which sloped steeply down at each side. At the extreme apex though, we observed with fascination that there was a flat ridge, about the width of the span of a woman's hand. My mother probably had hands that wide.

As I
With madness
Climbed the parapet
To put myself in space
And feeling then
The scrape of fear
The lonely kernel's wick
Of terrifying life............

These were words I wrote thirty years later in a poem when I tried to capture the experience of climbing up on the parapet of Brunel's Clifton Suspension Bridge over the Avon Gorge, near Bristol. A few years before my sister Teresa died, she took us there, my youngest son Liam and me, to see the wonder of it. I quote them now because the words express most clearly the feeling I had then, all those years before, as we, Pauline and I with madness, of joint mind, levered ourselves up, such tender ten year olds, to stand upright, thirty feet above the ground, our feet balanced carefully on the narrow, flat, baize-covered strip that stretched ahead of us for fifty feet, the whole length of the school hall beneath. The scrape of fear was just tingling the flesh. We walked confidently forward, arms outstretched on either side, heads high in the posture practised so often on the bars of my beloved Sandpit Park. A few words only, exchanged; "We'll get to the end".

And so we continued, Pauline and I. Triumphant, exhilarated, concentrated, totally mad. Mr Lilley, I am sure, did not intend this outcome to all his inspired teaching for the scholarship. The successful arrival at our destination (the end of the roof) was to be our downfall (but thank God in His heaven, not literally.) Standing aloft and overlooking the road and pavements of Hill Street, we saw to our consternation that a large crowd of people had gathered and were looking up at us. There was a frightening hush of sound. Or should I say absence of sound? The reality of our enterprise suddenly hit home. The scrape of fear such as I was to experience decades later on Avon suspension bridge became the pain of an unbearable, bleeding wound of terror.

As if drained of strength and with liquefying bones

we both sank in wordless unison, to a sitting position our legs straddling the roof. We turned our direction clumsily so that we were facing back the way we had come. But not before we had seen the blue helmets of two "coppers" amidst the crowd. Horror joined the tumult of emotions raging inside me. Not even my brothers, not even John, had brought a policeman to our door. Not a word from the coppers was spoken though. Just that terrifying hush.

No "Hello, Hello, Hello!" Maybe, unspoken, "Goodbye alas, Goodbye!"

Now came the long painful battle to return. Familiar words rang in my head.

"If you can keep your head when all about you Are losing theirs and blaming it on you" ....with good cause I add in retrospect. Once more the familiar words returned:

If you can force your heart and nerve and sinew.
To serve their turn long after they are gone,
And still hold on when there is nothing in you,

Except the will that says to you "Hold on." Hold on we did, Pauline and I, returning, slowly, laboriously, diminishing every second in self-belief and even hope. Terrified every second of the way. Kipling or no Kipling. Endless, endless journey. We felt like flies on the flank of a whale.

At the bottom of the ladder, as, like robots, we completed our journey, there stood the two helmeted representatives of the law ready to confront us. In spite of all my terror I immediately sensed by some strange inspiration, the best strategy to escape the worst consequences of our foolhardy enterprise. My family could be utterly disgraced. Why spoil the ship for a ha'porth of tar. Remember, I told you before how thin and small I was for my age. Once when Pauline and I had weighed ourselves, she was five stone six pounds and I was only three-stone-twelve. Now for once I could convert my weakness into strength! I sensed, in the incredulity and shock of the coppers, a measure of pity. I burst into convincing tears. I pleaded how sorry I was, I would never do it again, neither would Pauline, who stood astonished at my babbling performance.

I probably meant part of this rebuttal, but my main task now, I knew was to look like innocence itself, abject and totally submissive. Foolish but infinitely pitiable. At the same time sweet and quite adorable. One of them rumpled my hair as I sobbed,

"Please don't tell them, please don't tell them!" I knew we'd won when they began to smile. There were plenty of stern warnings accompanied by a postscript of sobs from me before they left us in the playground to see to the dispersal of the crowd. It was fortunate for us that there were no mobile phones in those days, neither was it an era when the public were hungry for sensation. There had been more than enough of that in the blitz of 1941. Helen and Margaret Croker were still at their prayers to Our Lady in the Church. They wouldn't know anything about it all. Our escapade would remain a secret. Was it the prayers of Helen and Margaret unbeknown to them, that saved us, perhaps?

The word then, never did get to our parents about our crazy, dangerous adventure. What did it all mean? Did it say something about our growing ambition and our desire to rise in the world? Via the scholarship perhaps? Or was it just something any kid might do faced with the temptation of a handy ladder?

19

Waiting...... Waiting...
"Only a sweet and virtuous soul,"

The second significant memory from this time of waiting and tension was one very private to me and revealed only to my mother, and now to you. I developed a fantasy that I had nearly passed the scholarship, but not quite. These penetrating examiners, before allowing me the privileges of a Grammar school education, would need from me some further proof of excellence. Unsurprisingly, thinking of excellence, my thoughts turned to poetry. Those faceless figures, to be convinced of my worth, would expect me to recite some beautiful poem. Accordingly, I scoured my few books.

Such a lovely poem, I found, so melodic. so sad, so full of yearning and nostalgia. It was true to the melancholic strain that was part of my character. It spoke too of the land I had left, whose loss deep inside I had assimilated from my parents – perhaps most of all from my father's nightly flute playing. The poem was called, "The Harper" and was written by Thomas Campbell. It begins:

> *On the green banks of Shannon when Sheila was nigh,*
> *No blithe Irish lad was as happy as I,*
> *No harp like my own could so cheerily play.*

And wherever I went was my poor dog Tray

The poem continues to tell the story of how the young man Pat, is parted from his beloved Sheila to seek a new life in England with only the company of "Poor dog Tray." True to tragic Irish tradition Pat fails in his efforts to secure this Nirvana, these pavements paved with gold, and it is only the steadfast love and loyalty of his dog that gives him some comfort. Sadly, the poem ends when poor dog Tray dies, and Pat gives voice to his despair and hopelessness:

Where now shall I go, poor, forsaken and blind,
Where find one to guide me so faithful and kind,
To my sweet native village so far, far away,
I will never more return with my poor dog Tray.

Having learned the poem by heart, I approached my mother as she washed the clothes in the kitchen. The kids played outside. I confided my plan. I don't know if she recognised it as my fantasy or thought in fact that this was a regulatory, scholastic requirement. So many things were a mystery to her in this strange English education, and she was wont to accept our assurances. Whichever the understanding, she took my request seriously and listened to my performance. I tell you it would have made a stone weep! But when I turned to look at her disappointed face, I could see only concern and deep worry.

"Isn't it a lovely poem itself," she said, "but you know...you know... it's too Irish. Why would those gentlemen want reminding of the terrible things that happened in the times of famine to those poor fellows who came to England without a coat to their back and no one to help them if they fell ill and died on the roadside. And things far worse happening in their own country if they didn't leave ......" She paused for a while and I could tell she had a whole lot more she could say,

"You'd be far better off choosing a poem that doesn't mention Ireland at all – you don't talk so thick anyway, so perhaps they wouldn't guess." (I think she forgot I was called O' Brien.)

To me it seemed a strange request. Did it really matter who the poor blind beggar was or where he came from, and didn't everyone love a dog? (Not me though, they still scared me after that baby accident). I was obedient though to the wisdom of my mother and I looked again at my books. and found a poem by George Herbert a favourite of mine to this day. It was called "Virtue." It is so well known and has been set to music too by some famous composer. I'm sure you know it, but if you don't I hope you enjoy:

Sweet day so cool so calm so bright,
The bridal of the earth and sky,
The dew shall weep thy fall tonight,
For you must die.

Sweet rose, whose angry hue and brave,
Bids the rash gazer wipe his eye,
Thy root is ever in thy grave,
For thou must die.

Sweet Spring, full of sweet days and roses,
A box where sweets compacted lie.
My music tells you have your closes
And thou must die.

Only a sweet and virtuous soul,
Like seasoned timber never gives,
And though the whole world turns to stone,
Then chiefly lives.

I write these words now as they come to my mind and I remember, as clear as day, my mother's approval and how convinced I was too that this was a vastly improved choice of poem for those discerning phantom examiners. Didn't it remind one of how everything in life, no matter how beautiful, could not escape mortality but what a great wonder it was that a little human soul, good and virtuous, was the only exception to this relentless rule and would never die or see decay.

Whilst embarked on a foolish enterprise I had been led to one of the most profound lessons of my life. And my mother in her wisdom knew this. I was never to be summoned to this fantasy ordeal nor scrutinised by these phantom examiners. I forgot all my misgivings and my mother was swallowed up once more in the thousand tasks of motherhood. But still deep in my heart was planted that hope, that not only would I pass the scholarship, I would also remain "A sweet and virtuous soul." And strong, like seasoned timber.

20
The Scholarship Results
"Well worth the sacrifice of chips"

It was a day I think in July when school had broken up. Not a summery day but overcast with cloud and threatening rain. All of us kids were standing round the table in the kitchen or maybe I had one of the few seats because I remember my chair being grabbed. This happened after a knock came to the kitchen door. No one ever knocked except at the front door. We were eating our chips for lunch, perhaps with some scratchings too, or even a scallop, but they were still on the newspaper to keep them warm, and the plate under.

My mum went to open the door. Imagine the surprise to see on the doorstep the tall, handsome figure of Mr. Lilley, our teacher, surrounded by about four grinning faces-faces of my classmates. "I've come to tell you", said Mr Lilley, "that Christine has passed her scholarship". The pupils gave a great "Whoop!" I could see then that my friend Pauline Croker was a member of the grinning company. Mr Lilley was smiling at me.

"You and Pauline have won a place at the finest girl's Grammar school in Coventry, Barr's Hill. This lot have passed too, two to Stoke Park girl's grammar and the two boys to the Technical college!" At this they all gave another whoop of joy.

"To celebrate," Mr Lilley continued, "we've got lemonade and crisps. Are you coming?" That's when someone in my family grabbed the chair from under me and I can remember the delighted faces of my little brothers as they swooped upon my barely touched chip portion.

"Can I have them? Can I have them?" rang in my ears, as appetite completely gone, I joined the happy throng outside and went goodness knows where, to celebrate what we could not yet possibly understand. I can't remember what was said to my poor mother, over-faced as she was by the presence of authority in her humble kitchen. She probably grabbed a flannel to wipe my face and straightened my plaits as I joined the triumphant gang. She would probably have reacted with dignity to shake Mr Lilley's hand as he left, smiling. He, no doubt, would have been luxuriating in the thought that he was now laying the foundations for his brave, new world – Coventry was rising from the ashes after the blitz of the war, and moreover it was to be the most rejected, the most ignominious, the Irish Catholics who were destined to play an important role in that remarkable recovery. For the first year in living memory more than one child from Saint Osburg's had passed the scholarship. Anyone seeing us though, would have "tutted" at the way we filled the pavements as we riotously passed, to drink our pop in the nearest park.

It wasn't long however, before I had intimations of the pains that lay ahead for me. I had passed the scholarship, and Helen, so much brighter, had not. I was two years younger, often considered a bit scatty, certainly young and naïve for my age and was often kept in line by my sister when it came to practical matters. What did she feel now? I know it must have been profound sadness, disappointment, humiliation, jealousy, helplessness and perhaps even despair. How do I know? I know because I felt that she felt them. In my bones I could sense the pain of all these emotions, All the grief of the first two failures in scholarship exams two years before would have been reactivated, and worse still the pleasures and rewards and honours and praise of passing the scholarship would have been blazoned before her eyes by the very sight of my scrawny frame. Even worse for me was to entertain the guilty feeling, that regardless of how keenly I regretted her predicament, I could not bring myself to wish it otherwise. I could not have sacrificed my own chance to go to Grammar school.

The extraordinary machinations of preparing for this new school added to the trauma for her. School uniform grants for poor children helped, but the major shopping trips and expenses for the long and foreign lists of requirements upset the whole household. Mum was away for long periods with me in tow to frequent some of the most prestigious school outfitters in Coventry's Broadgate.

Lady Godiva naked on her horse nearby, clothed only in her beautiful, blond hair, would have reflected with relief that her wardrobe problems were so simple when compared to the convolutions I was being exposed to in my preparations to become the typical English Grammar school girl, a cut above the riff-raff, and destined for a high role in society. After all you had to look the part!

You'll forgive, I'm sure this slight anachronism for the Lady Godiva statue that stands in Broadgate today, in 2018, was in fact installed in 1949 – a year after this shopping trip took place. For non-Coventrians who read this, this lovely statue was erected in honour of the historic courage of Godiva, wife of the cruel and heartless Earl Leofric who in the fourteenth century taxed his Coventry citizens to the point of starvation. In response to the pleas for help from the poor people his wife, the beautiful and virtuous Godiva, pleaded with her husband to have mercy on them. In the face of his cold refusal the sweet lady vowed she would ride naked through the city as a protest against his harshness. The word spread quickly through the poor people that in order to spare Godiva embarrassment everyone would sequester themselves indoors and not look upon her nudity. In the event, Godiva, as Tennyson records:

Rode forth clad only in her hair and her modesty.

I will include this lovely poem by Tennyson that commemorates this famous story in my epilogue at the end of my story. He wrote it after he passed once through Coventry station and was told of the famous legend. Only one citizen, it is said, failed to keep the embargo and looked out upon the naked lady. He was a fellow shamed now for all time and reviled by the name of "Peeping Tom." Nowadays when on the hour by the Broadgate clock a little Statue of Godiva naked on her horse, emerges to trot past, the sharp and spiteful little face of Peeping Tom emerges above her. Needless to say the husband Earl Leofric was so moved and ashamed, he immediately rescinded the taxes and the people lived happily after. To this day Godiva's name has been revered, her deeds captured in poetry by Tennyson and her beauty the subject of many a painting. Maybe the erection of her statue so soon after the ending of war was the city's defiant attempt to validate once again the virtues of courage, of humility and the inevitability of evil's defeat by the power of good. That just as Godiva's courage and virtue defeated and reformed the greed and cruelty of her husband so too the City of Coventry, in courage and virtue, would rise above the barbarity of those cruel attacks by the enemy in World War II.

But we must return with a sigh to the saga of Chrissie's outrageous shopping expeditions for clothes to attend Grammar school. Bendall's was the designated shop to purchase uniform. No other shop would do. No "two for one" offers from cheaper supermarkets in those days. Disbelief stuns me to this day as I think back to the prices of the garments and translate them now to their equivalence in the rent we paid for our house in Vincent street. A winter coat, of fine wool, £5, or ten weeks of rent, a velour bowler hat, £2 and ten shillings, five rent days, The hat band, two shillings and sixpence and the enamel hat badge the same again, another five rent days. And there was still the gym slip, the two blouses, winceyette for warmth (and expense), the navy blue long-legged knickers that doubled for P.E. (two pairs), gym blouse, (name embroidered in blue on the right hand breast side, at private expense), socks that reached to the knee and matching garters, outdoor sturdy shoes, indoor softer shoes and plimsolls – the obligatory hockey boots could be deferred a year (and the stick and pads). A cardigan too was an optional, but it was preferable to have a blazer, which would cover both winter and summer requirements. Extra money was needed for the Barr's Hill logo to be sown on to the breast pocket. There was also the shoe bag in regulation colours and material, which added another rent day or two to the tally. This too had to have your full name embroidered in large letters across it, in chain stitch. My mother had never heard of chain stitch, but fortunately a kind teacher, Miss O'Sullivan, at Saint Osburg's offered to do the embroidery for us and save me from shame. All of these clothes were in navy and sky blue and throughout the town Barr's Hill girls could be recognised by these colours, always walking like ladies, no more than two abreast on the pavement, never running and never, never eating in the street.

Imagine my mother's consternation when she was faced with all this expense, the poor children's uniform grant helped. My dad did over-time and I suspect Father Griffin did some sly transactions, because he called at our house a few times then, but somehow or other the uniform was purchased, and several shop keepers made a good profit. My mother was warned that the summer uniform would require two pin-striped dresses and most expensive of all a genuine Panama hat, plus band and badge. She deferred that worry to another day. In all this the required leather satchel for the transport of homework was totally forgotten.

So it was that I was equipped. My pain and mortification dug deep as, to an audience of interested neighbours, I was dressed in the kitchen in my posh attire. Helen looked on. It made me so unhappy that she wasn't beside me, dressed to the nines just as we had stood so often together to be admired, in our best white dresses with ringlets in our hair for the May and October processions for Our Lady. (Just as years later Helen and I had stood proudly side by side in our pale lavender bridesmaid dresses for

John's wedding to Anne when he was twenty-two!)

It seems hard to believe that with all this provocation Helen never said a word to show her pain and disappointment. Only now can I salute her amazing self-possession and unselfishness that she in no way made me feel uncomfortable. I did feel sad though that she seemed to develop a habit of decrying her own very considerable abilities. It probably helped a lot that she was soon to enter puberty and a foreign, adult world would open to her, far removed from the concerns of "little, childish, Chrissie." She was also within a couple of years to enter Underwood's secretarial college, paid for by my parents, to learn shorthand and typing, at which she immediately excelled. It equipped her to gain much desired employment as a private secretary in the civil service at Coventry's HMS Tax Office, 2, Far Gosford Street.

The neighbours "Oohed" and "Ah...hed" to see all my finery and I only wished that I could grow a little bigger to deserve such adulation. I questioned in my mind how I could possibly do justice to all these expectations. Was Barr's Hill Grammar School for Girls a step too far for me?

21

Barr's Hill Grammar School for Girls
"Arduus ad Astra"

Barr's Hill Grammar School for girls was situated on the Radford road. You could approach it from the city centre by walking up Bishop street from Corporation Street where all the buses passed on their way to Pool Meadow, or by traversing the long, once-genteel Middleborough road from the direction of Saint Osburg's Church, or from the direction of the Coundon district. This latter route along Middleborough road, passing high walls in ancient stone, was my favourite route and you could glimpse through tall, iron gates, large, mysterious houses, apparently empty and neglected and almost smothered by their overgrown gardens. It was a route that prepared us a little for the Victorian charm of Barr's Hill school itself. I say "us" because for a few weeks my friend Pauline prevailed on me to make a lengthy detour from my home, to meet at her house in Coundon, so that we could go to our new school together. We were to be the "Fuzzers" of the school and hence due for close inspection from all the older pupils, (we had been warned of this by an ex-pupil), but next year, she comforted, on seeing our dismay, we would be slightly less vulnerable as seasoned "Scrubbers".

The school itself was the converted Victorian home

of a man called James Kemp Starley, the nephew of James Starley, the famous man who invented the Penny Farthing bicycle and various tricycles, one of which was purchased by Queen Victoria herself. What was less well known though, was that the most famous bicycle of all, and the very prototype of all our modern bikes, "The Rover Safety Cycle" was the brainchild of his young nephew, James Kemp Starley. The safety bike became enormously successful and it was with money from this enterprise that he bought Barr's Hill House for his wife and ten children in 1889. After his death at an early age, his company went on to produce the Rover cars. Evidence of all these developments can be seen if you are interested, in Coventry's beautiful Motor Museum in the town centre. In later years the house of this man, who has been so neglected by posterity, was purchased by the local authority and converted into the first girl's grammar school in the city. (James Kemp Starley alas, had died young and there was never a mention of him and his substantial achievements, largely, people said, because he had been confused with his uncle, James Starley senior who had received all the acclaim.) "One more flower born to blush unseen," as the poet would say.

Two boys' independent grammar schools already existed in the city, one of which, King Henry VIII's, had stood for four hundred years, built with money gleaned from the dissolution of the monasteries. The very names of

Coventry landmarks remind one of how deeply religious the city had been and how much it had been impoverished by King Henry's cruel vandalism. Grey Friar's Green. White Friars, Black Friars ... all were obliterated from the city along with the reputedly splendid cathedral of Saint Mary's whose great spire had stood alongside those of the Cathedral of Saint Michael's and of Trinity Church in Broadgate, earning Coventry the title of the City of the three Spires. It is still honoured with that title to this day although people assume that the third spire must have been the much shorter one of Christ Church near the Central Hall and the Bull yard. It wasn't of course. It is especially poignant to learn from historians that Saint Mary's Cathedral was only destroyed on a selfish whim of Henry's because he had a grievance against the then provost. Earlier the king had vowed that although he would destroy all religious establishments because of their corruption, he would leave unharmed all churches and cathedrals. I suppose sparing some money for the establishment of the boy's grammar school of King Henry VIII gave a little ease to his conscience!

The other boys grammar school, Bablake School for Boys had been established even earlier, gifted by Isabel of France, the wife of King Edward II and reputed to be one of the oldest schools in the whole of England but now, in 1908, momentously, with the establishment of Barr's Hill Grammar School, girls were being considered as worthy candidates for higher education, and hence for schooling.

Imagine then, Pauline and I arriving at this august and historical mansion for our first Christmas term in 1948, as "Fuzzers" of the prestigious Barr's Hill Grammar School for Girls. We were laden on that mild September day with heavy woollen overcoats, velour bowler hats, bedecked with bands and badges, satchels, shoe-bags containing indoor shoes and plimsolls, and P.E. kit. We wore thick grey woollen socks held up to the knee with garters. Like two little donkeys we approached the wide, open, imposing gates and walking up the long winding drive, passed the ornate front door through which only teachers could enter. As inconspicuously as possible we crept in through what would once have been the servants' entrance and were directed to cloakrooms where we divested of our outer garments and changed to our indoor shoes, presumably to reduce the transmission of dirt from the streets, many of which were still scattered with the debris of bombing.

Inside the school the original structure of a gentleman's residence had been preserved. Downstairs rooms and corridors remained as in the original house, but were now converted into classrooms, art rooms and labs. You mounted to the upstairs rooms by wide and beautiful staircases, divided by a landing and flanked on each side by polished bannisters, perfect for a speedy descent. (I remember these same stairs were used by Miss Black our science teacher to illustrate the concept of horse power, By her calculation, having run up and down at my utmost speed I was given the score of one horse power. The results were somewhat skewed by my tendency to leap down four or five steps at a time rather than waste time on individual prancing!) A separate block had been built in the grounds of the house to accommodate extra classrooms, music rooms and a second gymnasium. The first gym in the main house was no more than a big room for simple exercises whereas the second had parallel bars and ropes and all sorts of climbing apparatus. This block was approached by a covered way and on either side were cultivated gardens, tennis and netball courts. Most fascinating of all was a rose-bedecked, enchanting staff garden where young teachers were seen to romantically stroll, and whose pretty lawns were never to my knowledge polluted by the step of a pupil. Thick shrubbery descended to a large hockey pitch which was especially memorable because if you progressed to the far border of the field you could see across the adjoining Naul's Mill park, the grounds of the equally prestigious independent grammar school for boys, Bablake. It had the same status as King Henry's. Many girls clustered at this border of bushes and shrubbery to gaze across the park, at muscular boy students, as they rolled in the mud of their rugby pitch. I could never understand the excitement of the girls. Perhaps with six brothers of my own to survey at home a little of the mystique of the male had been worn away.

All the lessons I loved at Barr's Hill and most of the teachers. Miss Hancock with her huge beehive of pink hair, taught us Latin and regularly accused us of being cabbages. She was a most dramatic teacher. In a tirade of abuse, her face an apoplectic pink, she berated her pupils for their lethargy and simple-mindedness. She would sometimes turn to me on the front row and say "I don't include you Christine, because I know you're sensitive like me and blush," and I would look at her purple face and blush even more. Her Latin results were always excellent. She walked along a little like a railway engine, sweeping aside any unfortunate child who got in her way.

Miss Weber who taught maths could be equally scathing of our intellectual abilities and would cover the blackboard with the workings of a sum, demanding of the girls, "Silly girls! Try to understand! Now watch the board while I go through it." Fortunately, her back was turned long enough for most of us to regain some composure from our suppressed giggles at the picture conjured up of Miss Weber's ample posterior disappearing into the algebraic equation. The maths was unknown to me and very difficult, but in a very short time her reassurances of her conviction in my abilities began to bear fruit and maths became an adventure. As long as I put down my legs and put on my glasses, I could do no wrong for her.

P.E. and English were my favourite lessons of all. The P.E. teacher, Miss Palmer, was rumoured to be well into her sixties and amused us by regularly withdrawing a large white hankie from its hiding place in her dark green knickers' leg and blowing her nose before replacing it. That the knickers' leg was surmounted by a dinky little, green, frilled, gym skirt made her actions seem even more incongruous. The knickers were the exact replica in style to our own capacious undergarments in dark navy blue, and we queried amongst ourselves whether other teachers had similar underclothing. She was a brisk and effective teacher and although at that stage we couldn't progress to apparatus work we worked hard to win the reward of a green gym stripe that was sown on our tunic, alongside the red posture stripe earned if teachers considered that you stood up straight enough "at all times." You see grammar schools were still redolent in those days of many military practices. Now at this moment of writing, recovering from a spinal injury, my doctor's advice to stand up as straight as possible at all times reminds me fondly of that proud day in the first term when I was one of the very few new girls to be awarded my red posture stripe, my first tangible reward at Barr's Hill Grammar School.

The English teachers in that first year and for several years after, were characterised for some unknown reason by having poor class control. Miss Settle, Miss

Prestige, and many others. They didn't seem to last so long. Perhaps the typical grammar schoolgirls in those days were lacking in their appreciation of a subject that didn't have a discernible relevance in the everyday world? Had war diminished the capacity for imagination and dreams? Or perhaps they hadn't been schooled as we had been at Saint Osburg's in so much poetry and reading. In spite of this class disorder though, I loved the English lessons. There was a new poetry book given out each term and I would immediately take it home and devour its contents the very first evening. Because I was the only child in the family with homework requirements, I was given the privilege of doing my studies in the "front" room – the best room, the same one that became my parents' bedroom when the bed-settee was opened. I had the privacy then to read all the new poems aloud and revel in the stories they told or the emotions they evoked. I surely learned to love the sound of my own voice. I'm certain it was that practice then that prepared me for the role of Eucharistic reader at Church when I was well in my sixties. Poetry too I realised had the uncanny knack of revealing some wise and perceptive observation about life that was almost like the tenets of religion in its enlightenment or in its power to provoke thought or guide action. This is what I truly thought then, but recently in the novel the "The Human Factor" by Grahame Green, I read, "There are verses in childhood...... which shape one's life more than any of the scriptures". I was amazed to learn that someone else was putting into words the insights of that ten-year old child. In English also there was a new novel to read every term, as well as stories and essays to write. One favourite lesson was when we had the freedom to find a favourite poem and copy it into a personal anthology in our best handwriting. I remember the first poem I copied. "The Blind Boy" by Colley Cibber, (another Victorian morality tale of overcoming disability and rejoicing in life's blessings.) It begins,

Oh say what is that thing called light,
Which I can ne'er enjoy? What are the blessings of the sight?
 Oh tell your poor blind boy.

After a long consideration of this question the little boy is comforted and after counting all his hitherto ignored blessings he concludes,

While thus I sing,
 I am a king
Although a poor blind boy.

This poem too I will include in my epilogue. Maybe I convince myself that you the reader will be equally enamoured of the poems I loved as a child but I suspect I was smitten with that universal compulsion to copy something that is greatly loved as if to make it one's own. Many, many more poems were copied carefully into my poetry anthology, with the devotion of a Medieval monk. By writing and decorating them I was taking them ever more deeply into my being.

You will be thinking there must also have been a great deal of the grammatical analysis of the mechanics of various styles of English, so intrinsic to a Grammar school education. It seemed like stuff that whilst ponderous to understand was very easy to forget, and completely unnecessary to remember. It also seemed a price worth paying for all the other delights of wonderful, wonderful English. I could continue for a long time recounting all the riches of the curriculum in that first year of Grammar school. Why, then, oh why, should pains arise in my mind in the telling?

Like the little mermaid of Hans Anderson, whose price for the sight of her beloved prince was to walk always on the cutting points of knives, so I was doomed to suffer my pains for a prize equally adored. How exaggerated, you might think, how melodramatic even narcissistic to make such a comparison. If that is so I have no excuse. That was the child I was. That was the person I was becoming.

22

Alienation, Two-fold
"Where do I belong?"

What were these pains then but the results of a two-fold alienation? Such a big word to use for a little girl's experience. I'm sure I didn't know the word in 1948. Maybe only Communists knew it. One aspect of it for me, was that

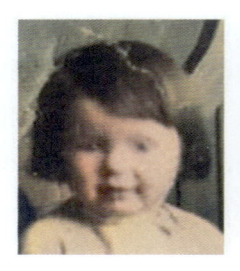

in my school-loving, studious, intellectually hungry self I began to feel a growing separation from my family, my neighbourhood and from all my "Up the Top" friends. But not, thank God, from my dear Catholic faith. It wasn't that these people were not still the core of my childhood life and absorbed time and energy and laughter, but now I found I was experiencing and learning so much that I just could not share. No one I knew at home understood French, or Science, or Geography, or History, or proper Latin. Neither did they do hard mathematical homework or understand that you can only draw a margin in pencil, not in ink. If I loved all these things, I was learning why couldn't I share my joy in them? Pauline had been assigned to a different class and we grew apart in things that mattered so I couldn't even share this anxiety with her.

Remember there were no TV sets in those days full of educational programmes and teeming with knowledge. Radios too were scarce. The few around worked on something called an accumulator, a heavy glass box filled with liquid chemicals that needed recharging every week or so at a local garage. Old Mr. Butler in the Thomas street court had one but they said, when my brothers called to play with his son Peter, old man Butler had chased them all away so that he could listen to the news. It was several years before my own family purchased a wireless set (on hire purchase no less, as I've mentioned already, because it was such a daring purchase), so there was understandably a certain suspiciousness about knowledge that was not transmitted orally or via the newspaper (but not the "News of the World.") I make an exception in recognising the information gleaned from the growing craze of the cinema, or the "flicks" as we called them, but since we children were fed mainly on the diet of "The Chum's Club" (every Saturday morning for 6d) life was not a source of knowledge like school, but full of laughs – mostly belly-laughs – with Old Mother Riley, The Three Stooges, Abbot and Costello, Laurel and Hardy, and Charlie Chaplin as the chief attractions. Big favourites also were the stylised Westerns, where the cowboys always wore white Stetsons and rode white horses. The cowboys were always very tall too and handsome, but they said Alan Ladd was filmed standing on an orange box because he wasn't tall enough. It wasn't as if I was persecuted on account of my increasing knowledge or desire for learning. To one boy from "Up the Top" who hailed my approach with, "Here comes the book worm!" I smartly and promptly replied, "Well it's better than being an ordinary worm!" and all the other kids had laughed at him. I remember it clearly because it was so rare for me to speak a word in self-defence. No, if there was persecution on that score, it came from myself. I suffered greatly to be learning so much that I couldn't talk about it with others.

There was however in my neighbourhood a strong sense of repugnance with regard to the uniform I wore. Can you blame those critics? After years of scrabbling for clothes on clothing coupons, unpicking woollies to knit new ones in Fair-isle and fighting to get hold of parachute remnants to make petticoats or even dresses, what an affront it must have been to see the quality and style of all my posh garb. As for the velour bowler hat, bedecked with ribbon and shiny badge, its incongruity in our poor streets would be equalled today by a young lady walking the East End of London in a Victoria Beckham evening gown with a bejewelled crown on her head!

Trouble was no surprise then, but some experiences

cut deeper than others. For instance, returning home from school via Trafalgar Street I always clung to the pavement, which was flanked by small factories, not houses. I had come home already avoiding the bomb craters of Windsor street and travelling up medieval Spon street (what was left of it) I had turned off at Hope street where in the dirt of the pavement several little toddlers played daily, clad only in vests. Once in Trafalgar Street on the opposite pavement I knew, lurked a wolfish housewife who stood at her door awaiting my passage. With malicious joy she would yell as I approached,

"Here come that bloody bugger, with her bloody, big hat!"

That persistent abuse hurt far more than that which I received less frequently from an equally vicious housewife who timed my passing as I went up Thomas Street to collect the daily bread after school. This day I was dressed only in gym tunic and school blouse. As I passed, she several times threw with considerable force, a bucket of dirty water to soak me from top to bottom. I heard that it was common practice in Dublin to throw your slops into the street so we reassured ourselves that it may not have been personal. Enough though was said in furtive glances and sneaky whispers for me to get the message that I could no longer be totally accepted in my neighbourhood. I could never again be a bono-fide member of my community. It was my own fault. Didn't I consider myself a cut above everyone else?

I learned my lesson well. Take great care lest you show any evidence of superiority!

I have just described one aspect of my alienation, the separation of my "English" schooling from my Irish community and family. The other aspect was the separation of my Irish, Catholic origins from the prevailing culture of my English, Protestant, Grammar school environment. In a school of about five hundred and fifty girls only thirty were Catholic. And even worse for the Jews who boasted only two. I know this precisely because each morning from the whole school assembly for prayers, Jews and Catholics were excluded and sent to an adjacent room where we could count ourselves to our hearts' content and reflect on our marginalised status. It wasn't just the fault of the school, which was strictly Church of England, but probably a requirement too of our own Catholic and Jewish faiths that we did not share worship with "Protestants". A sad measure of bigotry on both sides.

This exclusion did though have a particularly, painful effect. At the end of the morning religious ceremony the Headmistress Miss Barlow (and a Justice of the Peace) would give out notices to the staff and school, and these were often at great length. Badges, cups and certificates were distributed also and all the paraphernalia that recognised success or achievement. Obviously we thirty two dissenters couldn't be excluded from all this, but what I could never understand was that instead of allowing us to re-join the school discreetly at the rear of the big hall, we were ushered in at the very front of all the sitting pupils and watched over even more scarily by the ranks of staff members who were ensconced on either side of the Headmistress on a raised platform. We were scrutinised from the left and the right as we entered, in single file. No chance then to show one's better side! No pirate walking the plank could have felt the fear and self-consciousness that even daily custom failed to lessen.

You may remember earlier when I wrote of my mother's valiant efforts to equip me with the Barr's Hill uniform, she completely forgot the requirement of a good leather school satchel. Consequently, at the last minute we had improvised with the little money left with the purchase of a small frail suitcase with weak clips on either side of the handle and no lock. Because the clips didn't close firmly, I used to put my hand under the handle of the case and hold it shut manually. Yes! You've guessed it! As I walked into the Assembly one day my poor hand slipped and in full view of Headmistress, staff, school and even the others who walked with me, my case burst open and the whole of its contents spilled on the floor with a deafening clang. A thousand pencils scattered in every direction. I scrabbled on the floor to retrieve what I could. Someone must have helped me, but I can't tell you more because I've blocked it out.

For months afterwards though this gigantic faux pas was top of my bedtime list of the ways I was different from everyone else in that school. The rest of my list went something like this:

1) Only one other girl has a name beginning with O' (and she doesn't really count because she's your best friend at the moment and anyway she has an aunt who is a teacher who can embroider and can afford to pay for her niece's elocution lessons.)

2) Hardly anyone in school has red hair and just a few have plaits.

3) Hardly anyone is a Catholic and has to queue up separately for fish on Friday and get looked at crossly.

4) I'm one of the two in my class who can't join in Scripture lessons even though we always know all the answers about the New Testament and it sounds really interesting.

5) I don't know anyone else in the whole school who has eight children in her family and lives in such a small house. People I don't even know ask me about all these siblings but only to know where there is room is for them all to sleep.

6) No one I know has a dad who gets so dirty at work. (He had just started work labouring on the buildings). Poor dad, his boots were enormous. Worst of all I felt ashamed of him and I felt so guilty to feel ashamed.

Now after the disaster with the suitcase I added yet another grievance to my tally of sensitivities, the ones I pondered endlessly in my bed at night, repeating them like some dolorous rosary.

My childhood then at the age of twelve was coming to an end. James Barrie wrote once that "Nothing that happens after we are twelve matters very much" and although like Barrie the years ahead held many joys there was a sense always of some irrevocable loss. The glorious days of innocence were no more.

I was no longer my whole self. Could I ever be severed from my Catholic, Irish, immigrant identity; my Church, my Faith, my Lord; my mother, my father, my brothers and sisters – and although I couldn't know it then, the four more siblings who were to come? No, never. But likewise, could I ever be severed either from this fine Grammar school, from all my school subjects, from these concerned, inspiring and often in my case, indulgent teachers; from these dreams of going to university and becoming a writer or a journalist or perhaps a teacher?

Never. Never. Never. Could I ever be separated either from this ancient city of Coventry, once one of the few cities in England to boast two Cathedrals and dominated by a multitude of religious orders in the days before the Reformation. It was famous too throughout the centuries for its technical abilities, adapting as years passed from textiles and ribbon-making, to watch-making, to the munitions of the Second World War, and eventually becoming a world famous centre for the bicycle and the car industry. No, there must be a marriage here within me and whatever the cost I must pay, I must pay it. But never tell a soul.

23
Coda

When I first decided to tell the story of my childhood as a "Catholic, Irish, Immigrant Child", my main motivation, was to sing a song of praise and gratitude for my mother and father who brought us children up in such difficult circumstances. I wanted to tell the tale of an immigrant family in a land so foreign and I wanted at the same time to commemorate and celebrate the joyous strength and fortitude that was given to us all by our dear Catholic faith.

It was to recall too all the delights and joys of childhood experienced in those years of the 1940s and that wonderful capacity children had even in those days of war, to share in a culture of their own, so rich and gregarious. I wanted also to pay a tribute to the goodness of all the teachers and priests who touched upon and helped our family, most singularly of all, the Benedictine priest Father Basil Griffin and the demob-happy Mr. Lilley who were of such a transforming influence in all our lives, but mine in particular. There were so many other people to commemorate, too numerous to mention.

But now as I draw my story to a close, I realise that my story has been drawn on a wider canvas. Shining through all these minutiae of a little child's life, has been the story of Coventry city itself and its near miraculous survival from the utter devastation of the bombing and the Blitz. The marvel that so many lives were saved. That so many families like ours were rehoused repeatedly. That buildings were razed and rebuilt, that schools were repaired, churches restored, and education continued, even though limping at times. And not least of all the fact that factories reopened with barely a hitch to continue their sterling work supplying munitions and then, as the war ceased, transferring to car production so seamlessly in order to restore economic growth to the city and help subsidise the massive rebuilding of houses that was to take place in the early fifties. It was an effort that could now be so easily emulated in our time of housing crisis.

It was to one such rebuilt house erected by the builders, Wimpy, on the Tile Hill North estate that my family moved when I was fifteen to make room for our ever-increasing family. Now as I wander through that same estate at the age of eighty, having lived for twelve years in the north of England, in Manchester and then a nearby Lancashire mill village, and for twenty years in the far south of England on the coast of Hampshire, I marvel at the architects and designers who laid out in the 1950s such pleasing and spacious residences in that Tile Hill estate and preserved so much of the ancient woodland and trees.

George Shaw the artist, nominated for the Turner

prize in 2015, having grown up on this estate, captures the extraordinary appeal of that war-time achievement. Nominated for the Turner prize and having had an exhibition at the National Gallery Shaw celebrates the courageous spirit shown by Coventrians in the aftermath of war's destruction.

I could not tell my story without acknowledging my debt to this city. In the year when Coventry city has been nominated as City of Culture for 2021 perhaps it is salutary to be reminded of the huge obstacles that had to be overcome for the city to receive that honour. So that the Phoenix could rise even further from the ashes. And perhaps one day to fly high!

Shining even more brightly though, on that broad canvas that I wove with very little awareness of its foundational textures, is a theme of great relevance to our city. This is the theme of immigration. In spite of the war, in spite of evacuations and in spite of the hardships of injuries, food privations and dangerous illness, I never heard my parents utter a word of regret about their decision to move from Eire, to England, and to Coventry in particular. There was, I noticed in them, a palpable pride in making their contributions as citizens, if not as nationals. In the realm of work my father was proud to be able to contribute "for as many hours as God sends," as he would have phrased it, and to constantly supplement his income, to care for his large and constantly growing family. He was proud to be able to change his job whenever opportunities arose to make more money. This was especially true in the period outside the remit of my story when he took the opportunity to work as a sub-contractor in the building trade when Coventry began to be rebuilt, especially in the Eastern Green area of the city. That extra money was to help fund my university education, alongside the generous grant I received from my State Scholarship.

My mother surprised me sometimes by contrasting the "English" style priests like the Benedictines of Saint Osburg's favourably with their Irish counterparts, commenting on their readiness to enter the nitty-gritty of the lives of the poorest immigrant parishioners. Although devout in her faith and a woman reluctant to pass judgement, she spoke very disparagingly of the superior and judgemental style of the priests in Ireland, who sought out the company of rich parishioners. No piety had been lacking in Ireland but some of the clergy there were not true shepherds of their flocks, she claimed.

And I remember with the strongest affection my parents' reverence for the importance of my Grammar school education. Each pupil was given a report book, each term the teachers of the child would record a comment on progress or concern. At the bottom of the term's page was a place for a parental signature. As the new term was about to resume, with the seriousness of signing a marriage certificate, my father would find his best pen and summoning myself and my mother as witnesses he would sign the report with a flourish. *J O' Brien*. How I loved that little testimony, for he spoke little. I can remember no comments being made on the reports themselves. They were usually satisfactory with the occasional flash of approval. What I remember most clearly though was the look of quiet pride of a father that said his daughter was attending the best girls' Grammar school in Coventry!

We immigrants then were beginning to settle into their new nationality. They were beginning to be accepted all over the city. They were keeping their identity, their Catholic faith, their music, their Irish dancing, their wonderful humour and hospitality and the many other gifts they brought to life. Not least their readiness to work hard and tirelessly. Throughout the fifties and sixties how far did their kindly assimilation into Coventry life act as a template for all the waves of immigration which were yet to come to the city? There were arrivals from the Caribbean, those from Pakistan and India, and as the decades passed, the immigrants from so many African countries and latterly, Polish and East Europeans. And most recently the extraordinary generosity shown in the acceptance of Syrian refugees, more per capita than any other city in England. Neither should be forgotten the huge influx of foreign students to the greatly prospering universities of Warwick and Coventry. When Coventry was given its nomination as a future city of culture, in particular, it was praised for the successful integration of so many of its immigrants.

Did that first influx of so many Irish people in the pre-and post-war period enable this great achievement to take place? Coventry was long acknowledged as a "City of Reconciliation" and the statue in the ruins of the Old Cathedral reminds us of this. Was it with the acceptance of those poor Irish immigrants that the seeds of reconciliation were planted?

If so, how many more little immigrant children experienced the transition in the way that I did? And how praiseworthy must be all those worthy people who aided them and welcomed them in the huge task of assimilation that lay ahead.

Returning to the micro canvas though, one last time. In what way now, at eighty-two years of age, do I look back at my childhood? Sometimes, I envisage the statue that appeared in the dream of Nebuchadnezzar and was interpreted for the king by the prophet Daniel in the Old Testament. In the dream the king saw a statue composed of many different materials. The order of its composition in the biblical story is reversed for me. No head of gold now, with the graduated body of silver, thighs of bronze, lower legs of iron and feet of clay. Instead I visualise that in the statue of my life, my childhood were the golden foundations, silver, bronze, iron the years of my adulthood and now after decades of decreasing durability I exist with such a poor head of clay!

"And unto dust thou shall return" I remind myself, as Lent approaches heralded in by Ash Wednesday. Sometimes I envisage myself as Charles Causley's child in his poem:

Who is the Child I see Wandering, Wandering?

He asks repeatedly only to realise with a shock that that unrecognised child is indeed himself. I too, like Causley, often fail abjectly to recognise myself in the child I can so clearly recall. I identify myself too, but only in my most melancholy or guilt-ridden moments. As Hans Christian Anderson's Kay in the story of the Snow Queen who lost his loving heart as a splinter of ice fell into it. "Can I really love now as I did as a child?" I ask myself. "When will come my Gerda to believe in me and restore my lost humanity?"

And most melancholy of all in my most doleful mood do I recall Thomas Hood's "I Remember, I Remember" poem. The poet recalls some of the delights of his childhood, his original home, his tiny bedroom, the garden and its lovely flowers, But in spite of all these treasured memories of his childhood they are not enough to dispel his sad conclusion,

And now 'tis little joy,
To know I'm further off from heaven than when I was a boy

No, these are just the fancy ruminations which may all have some share of truth. And 'What is truth?' I ask like Pilate. Can one ever know one's life? No, of course not.

But maybe if you are lucky you might just capture some small part of it.

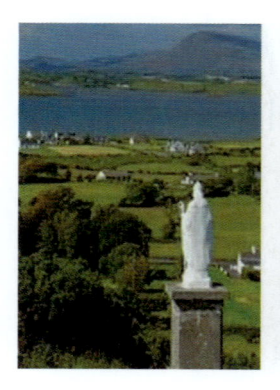

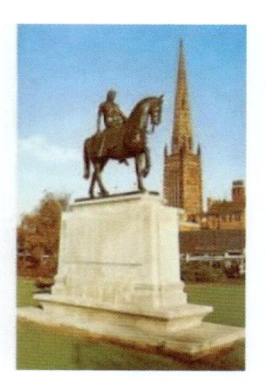

Annie Christina Knox, 2020

Epilogue – My Journey in Poems

Three Little Kittens

The three little kittens they lost their mittens,
And they began to cry,
Oh, mother dear, we sadly fear
Our mittens we have lost
What? Lost your mittens, you naughty kittens!
Then you shall have no pie.
Mee-ow, mee-ow, mee-ow.
We shall have no pie.
Our mittens we have lost.

The three little kittens they found their mittens,
And they began to smile,
Oh, mother dear, see here, see here,
Our mittens we have found
What? Found your mittens, you good little kittens,
And you shall have some pie.
Mee-ow, mee-ow, mee-ow.
We shall have some pie.
Let us have some pie.

The three little kittens put on their mittens,
And soon ate up the pie;
Oh, mother dear, we greatly fear
Our mittens we have soiled
What? Soiled your mittens, you naughty kittens!
Then they began to sigh,
Mee-ow, mee-ow, mee-ow.
Our mittens we have soiled.
Then they began to sigh.

The three little kittens they washed their mittens,
And hung them out to dry;
Oh! Mother dear, look here, look here,
Our mittens we have washed

What? Washed your mittens, you good little kittens,
But smell a rat close by.
Mee-ow, mee-ow, mee-ow.
We smell a rat close by.
Let's all have some pie.

The little Doll - Charles Kingsley

I once had a sweet little doll, dears,
The prettiest doll in the world;
Her cheeks were so red and so white; dears,
And her hair was so charmingly curled.

But I lost my poor little doll, dears,
As I played on the heath one day;
And I cried for more than a week, dears;
But I never could find where she lay.

I found my poor little doll, dears,
As I played on the heath one day;
Folks say she is terrible changed, dears,
For her paint is all washed away,

And her arm trodden off by the cows, dears,
And her hair not the least bit curled:
Yet for old sakes' sake she is still, dears
The prettiest doll in the world.

The Wreck of The Hesperus
- Henry Wadsworth Longfellow

It was the schooner Hesperus,
That sailed the wint'ry sea;
And the shipper had taken his little daughter,
To bear him company.

Blue were her eyes as the fairy-flax,
Her cheeks like the dawn of day,
And her bosom white as the hawthorn buds
That opens in the month of May.

The skipper he stood besides the helm,
His pipe was in his mouth,
And watched how the veering flaw did blow
The smoke now West, now South.

Then up and spake an old Sailor,
Had sailed the Spanish Main,
"I pray thee put into yonder port,
For I fear a hurricane.

"Last night, the moon had a golden ring,
And tonight no moon we see!"
The skipper, he blew a whiff from his pipe,
And a scornful laugh launched he.

Colder and louder blew the wind,
A gale from the North-east;
The snow fell hissing in the brine,
And the billows frothed like yeast.

Done came the storm, and smote amain
The vessel in its strength;
She shuddered and paused, like a frighted steed,
Then leaped her cable's length.

"Come hither! Come hither! My little daughter,

And do not tremble so;
For I can weather the roughest gale
That ever wind did blow."

He wrapped her warm in his seaman's coat
Against the stinging blast;
He cut a rope from a broken spar,
And bound her to the mast.

"O father! I hear the church-bells ring,
O say what may it be?"
"Tis a fog-bell on a rock-bound coast!"
And he steered for the open sea.

"O father! I hear the sound of guns,
O say what may it be?"
"Some ship is distress, that canot live
In such an angry sea!"

"O father! I see a gleaming light,
O say what may it be?"
But the father answered never a word,
A frozen corpse was he.

Lashed to the helm, all stiff and stark,
With his face turned to the skies,
The lantern gleamed through the gleaming snow
On his fixed and glassy eyes.

Then the maiden clasped her hands and prayed
That saved she might be;
And she thought of Christ who stilled the wave
On the Lake of Galilee.

And fast through the midnight dark and drear,
Through the whistling sleet and snow,
Like a sheeted ghost, the vessel swept
Towards the reef of Norman's Woe.

And ever the fitful gusts between

A sound came from the land;
It was the sound of the trampling surf,
On the rocks and the hard sea-sand.

The breakers were right beneath her bows,
She drifted a dreary wreck,
And a whopping billow swept the crew
Like icicles from her deck.

She struck where the white and fleecy waves
Looked soft as carded wool,
But the cruel rocks, they gored her sides
Like the horns of an angry bull.

Her rattling shrouds, all sheathed in ice,
With the masts went by the board;
Like a vessel of glass she stove and sank,
Ho! Ho! The breakers roared!

At daybreak, on the bleak sea-beach,
A fisherman stood aghast,
To see the form of a maiden fair
Lashed close to a drifting mast.

The salt sea was frozen on her breast,
The salt tears in her eyes;
And he saw her hair, like the brown seaweed,
On the billows fall and rise.

Such was the wreck of the Hesperus,
In the midnight and the snow!
Christ save us all from a death like this
On the reef of Norman's Woe!

Lord Ullin's Daughter - Thomas Campbell

A chieftain, to the Highlands bound,
Cries, "Boatman, do not tarry;
And I'll give thee a silver pound
To row us o'er the ferry."

"Now, who be ye, would cross Lochgyle,
This dark and stormy water?"
"O! I'm the chief of Ulva's isle,
And this, Lord Ullin's daughter.

"And fast before her father's men
Three days we've fled together,
For should he find us in the glen,
My blood would stain the heather.

"His horsemen hard behind us ride;
Should they our steps discover,
Then who will cheer my bonny bride,
When they have slain her lover?"

Out spoke the hardy Highland wight:
"I'll go, my chief - I'm ready:
It is not for your silver bright,
But for your winsome lady.

"And by my word! the bonny bird
In danger shall not tarry:
So, though the waves are raging white,
I'll row you o'er the ferry."

By this the storm grew loud apace,
The water-wraith was shrieking;
And in the scowl of heaven each face
Grew dark as they were speaking.

But still as wilder blew the wind,
And as the night grew drearer,

*Down the glen rode armed men
Their trampling sounded nearer.*

*"O haste thee, haste!" the lady cries,
"Though tempests round us gather;
I'll meet the raging of the skies,
But not an angry father."*

*The boat has left a stormy land,
A stormy sea before her,
When, O! too strong for human hand,
The tempest gather'd o'er her.*

*And still they row'd amidst the roar
Of waters fast prevailing:
Lord Ullin reach'd that fatal shore,
His wrath was changed to wailing.*

*For, sore dismay'd through storm and shade,
His child he did discover;
One lovely hand she stretch'd for aid,
And one was round her lover.*

*"Come back! Come back!" he cried in grief
"Across this stormy water;
And I'll forgive your Highland chief,
My daughter! – O my daughter!"*

*'Twas vain: the loud waves lash'd the shore,
Return or aid preventing;
The waters wild went o'er his child,
And he was left lamenting.*

Extract from Pilgrim's Progress by John Bungan

Far have I come laden with my sin
Nor could ought ease me of the grief that I was in
Till I come hither. What place is this?
Must here be the beginning of my bliss?
Must here the burden fall from my back?
Must here the strings that bound it to me crack?
Blest cross! Blest sepulchre!
Blest ever be, the man that there was put to death for me.

The Cripple Boy - John William Kneeshaw

There was a lonely cottage once
Upon a mountain side
And higher still above it rose
The summits in their pride.
A village in the valley lay
But that was far below
Whence all except the wild goats came
With weary step and slow.

A Widow owned that lowly hut,
She had one only joy
Alas her care and sorrow too,
He was A Cripple Boy.
He could not climb the mountain path,
He could not run nor play
Nor earn his daily bread for which
His Mother toiled all day.

"Oh Mother," he would sometimes say,
"Why has God made me so?
What use am I, what work is mine?"
And then the tears would flow.
"Nay nay my child be patient still
Be sure thy words are true.
God has a plan for every man
And he has one for you."

The souls of War were swelling then
Around that fair free land
But her sons had sworn that on her soil
No foeman's foot should stand.
And on each height a sentry stood
With keen unerring eye
The watch fires blazzed to kindle
Should the enemy surprise.

The cripple slept at midnight hour

Then woke he knew not why
A secret impulse called him forth
Beneath the starry sky.
Then led him up he knew not where
Until at last he stood
Upon the height beside the pile,
The final pile of wood.

There was no sentry at the post,
The place was lone and still,
Hush! Hark! See! See! Those stealing men,
Just creeping round the hill!
Now, cripple boy, there's work for you,
Your mother's words are true;
God has a plan for every man,
And he has one for you.

One moment and the flames burst forth,
They saw it, far and near
They saw it too those baffled foes
And knew their chances was o'er.
One shot they fired and down they went,
Back to their camp once more,
But where was he, the feeble child
So weak and yet so brave?

They bore him to his home at length,
There was triumph in his eye,
Saying - "Mother, dear, don't weep for me,
I'm happy thus to die;
I could not ask for longer life,
For I have lived to see,
God has a plan for every man,
And he had one for me."

John Peel – English Folk Song

Do ye ken John Peel with his coat so gay?
Do ye ken John Peel at the break of day?
Do ye ken John Peel when he's far, far away
With his hounds and his horn in the morning.

Twas the sound of his horn brought me from my bed
And the cry of his hounds has me oftimes led
For Peel's view holloa would wake the dead
Or a fox from his lair in the morning.

Do ye ken that hound whose voice is death?
Do ye ken her sons of peerless faith
Do ye ken that a fox with his last breath
Cursed them all as he died in the morning?

Yes, I ken John Peel and auld Ruby, too
Ranter and Royal and Bellman so true
From the drag to the chase, from the chase to the view
From the view to the death in the morning.

And I've followed John Pell both often and far
O'er the rasper fence and the gate and the bar
From Low Denton Holme to the Scratchmere Scar
When we vied for the brush in the morning.

Then here's to John Peel with my heart and soul
Come fill, fill to him a brimming bowl
For we'll follow John Peel thro fair or thro foul
While we're waked by his horn in the morning.

Early One Morning – English Folk Song

Early one morning,
Just as the sun was rising,
I heard a young maid sing,
In the valley below.

CHORUS:

Oh, don't deceive me,
Oh, never leave me,
How could you use
A poor maiden so?

Remember the vows,
That you made to your Mary,
Remember the bow'r,
Where you vowed to be true,

Chorus

Oh Gay is the garland,
And fresh are the roses,
I've culled from the garden,
To place upon thy brow.

Chorus

Thus sand the poor maiden,
Her sorrows bewailing,
Thus sang the poor maid,
In the valley below.

Chorus

Another version:

Early one morning
Just as the sun was rising,
I heard a young maid sing
In the valley below.

Oh, don't deceive me,
Oh, never leave me,
How could you use
A poor maiden so?

Remember the vows that
You made to me truly,
Remember how tenderly
You nestled close to me.

Gay is the garland
Fresh are the roses
I've culled from the garden
To bind over thee.

Here I now wander
Alone as I wonder
Why did you leave me
To sigh and complain.

I ask of the roses
Why should I be forsaken,
Why must I here in sorrow remain?
Through yonder grove by the spring that is
running,

There you and I have so merrily played,
Kissing and courting and gently sporting,
Oh, my innocent heart you've betrayed.
Soon you will meet with another pretty maiden,

Some pretty maiden,
You'll court her for a while.
Thus ever changing,
Always seeking for a girl that is new.

Thus sung the maiden,
Her sorrows bewailing
This sung the maid
In the valley below

Oh, don't deceive me,
Oh, never leave me,
How could you use
A poor maiden so?

Boots – Rudyard Kipling
(Infantry Columns)

We're foot--slog--slog--slog--sloggin' over Africa --
Foot--foot--foot--foot--sloggin's over Africa --
(Boots--boots--boots--boots--movin' up an' down again!)
  There's no discharge in the war!

Seven--six--eleven--five--nine-an'-twenty mile to-day --
Four--eleven--seventeen--thirty-two the day before --
(Boots--boots--boots--boots--movin' up an' down again!)
  There's no discharge in the war!

Don't--don't--don't--don't--look at what's in front of you.
(Boots--boots--boots--boots--movin' up an' down again);
Men--men--men--men--men go mad with watchin' em,
  An' there's no discharge in the war!

Try--try--try--try--to think o' something different --
Oh--my--God--keep--me from goin' lunatic!
(Boots--boots--boots--boots--movin' up an' down again!)
  There's no discharge in the war!

Count--count--count--count--the bullets in the bandoliers.
If--your--eyes--drop--they will get atop o' you!
(Boots--boots--boots--boots--movin' up an' down again)
  There's no discharge in the war!

We--can--stick--out--'unger, thirst, an' weariness,
But--not--not--not--not the chronic sight of 'em --
Boots--boots--boots--boots--movin' up an' down again,
  An' there's no discharge in the war!

"Taint--so--bad--by--day because o' company,
But night--brings--long--strings--o' forty thousand million
Boots--boots--boots--boots--movin' up an' down again.
  There's no discharge in the war!

I--'ave--marched--six--weeks in 'Ell an' certify
It--is--not--fire--devils, dark, or anything,
But boots--boots--boots--boots--movin' up an' down again,
  An' there's no discharge in the war!

If - Rudyard Kipling

If you can keep your head when all about you
Are you losing theirs and blaming it on you;
If you can trust yourself when all men doubt you,
Ut make allowance for their doubting too:
If you can wait and not be tired by waiting,
Or, being lied about, don't deal in lies,
Or being hated don't give way to hating,
And yet dont look too good, nor talk too wise;

If you can dream- -and not make dreams your master;
If you can think - -and not make thoughts your aim,
If you can meet with Triumph and Disaster
And treat those two impostors just the same:.
If you can bear to hear the truth you've spoken
Twisted by knaves to make a trap for fools,
Or watch the things you gave your life to, broken,
And stoop and build'em up with worn-out tools;

If you can make one heap of all your winnings
And risk it on one turn of pitch-and-toss,
And lose, and start again at your beginnings,
And never breathe a word about your loss:
If you can force your heart and nerve and sinew
To serve your turn long after they are gone,
And so hold on when there is nothing in you
Except the Will which says to them: 'Hold on!'

If you can talk with crowds and keep your virtue,
Or walk with Kings - nor lose the common touch,
If neither foes nor loving friends can hurt you,
If all men count with you, but none too much:
If you can fill the unforgiving minute
With sixty seconds' worth of distance run,
Yours is the Earth and everything that's in it,
And - which is more - you'll be a Man, my son!

On Clifton Bridge Over the Avon Gorge
– Christine Knox

Isambard Kingdom Brunel -
Two hundred feet above the Avon gorge
You scaped the Clifton Bridge -
From rocky cliff-face
To green and bushy clime,
Across the turgid, sluggish flow
Of river far below.

Trellis of steel you built,
Swooping, filigree - posted arch,
Fragile to the eye
As the spider's spun
Across my window pane.
My senses are upturned to step
So safely in the sky.

In eighteen hundred and sixty-four
How did you plan this feat?
From the scoured and flint-hard precipice
Did you spy the verdurous glade
As a distant paradise,
And decide like a bird you would fly
To the Garden of Eden beyond?

Or, seeing the mudflat and the ooze
Of dank and dirty estuary,
Did you accurse the primal slime
Of man's first begetting,
And swear of humankind more fit
To tread with gracious nobleness
The portals of the skies?

Or perhaps, like me, one April day
You stepped on lofty promontory -
As I, with madness, climbed the parapet
To put myself in space -

And feeling then, the scrape of fear,
The lonely kernel's wick
Of terrifying life

You said, "I'll build a bridge
So all will understand
To escape the sludge
And reach the arborous shore,
Man must suspended stand
Between life and death. Sky and earth.
My bridge will bring rebirth."

The Harper - Thomas Campbell

On the green banks of Shannon, when Sheelah was nigh,
No blithe Irish lad was so happy as I;
No harp like my own could so cheerily play,
And wherever I went was my poor dog Tray.

When at last I was forced from my Sheelah to part,
She said (while the sorrow was big at her heart),
"O, remember your Sheelah when far, far away;
And be kind, my dear Pat, to our poor dog Tray."

Poor dog! He was faithful and kind, to be sure,
And he constantly loved me, although I was poor;
When the sour-looking folks sent me heartless away,
I had always a friend in my poor dog Tray.

When the road was so dark, and the night was so cold,
And Pat and his dog were grown weary and old,
How snugly we slept in my old coat of gray,
And he licked me for kindness, my poor dog Tray.

Though my wallet was scant, I remembered his case,
Nor refused my last crust to his pitiful face;
But he died at my feet on a cold winter day,
And I played a sad lament for my poor dog Tray.

When now shall I go, poor forsaken, and blind?
Can I find one to guide me, so faithful and kind?
To my sweet native village, so far, far away,
I can nevermore return with my poor dog Tray.

Godiva - Alfred, Lord Tennyson

I waited for the train at Coventry;
I hung with grooms and porters on the bridge,
To watch the three tall spires; and there I shaped
The city's ancient legend into this:
Not only we, the latest seed of Time,
New men, that in the flying of a wheel
Cry down the past, not only we, that prate
Of rights and wrongs, have loved the people well,
And loathed to see them overtax'd; but she
Did more, and underwent, and overcame,
The woman of a thousand summers back,
Godiva, wife to that grim Earl, who ruled
In Coventry: for when he laid a tax
Upon his town, and all the mothers brought
Their children, clamoring, "If we pay, we starve!"
She sought her lord, and found him, where he strode

About the hall, among his dogs, alone,
His beard a foot before him and his hair
A yard behind. She told him of their tears,
And pray'd him, "If they pay this tax, they starve."
Whereat the stared, replying, half-amazed,
"You would not let your little finger arch
For such as these?" - "But I would die, " said she.
He laugh'd, and swore by Peter and by Paul;
Then filip'd at the diamond in her ear;
"Oh ay, ay, ay, you talk!" - "Alas!" she said,
"But prove me what I would not do."
And from a heart as rough as Esau's hand,
He answer'd, "Ride you naked thro' the town,
And I repeal it;" and nodding, as in scorn,
He parted, with great strides among his dogs.
So left alone, the passions of her mind,
As winds from all the compass shift and blow,
Made war upon each other for an hour,

Till pity won. She sent a herald forth,
And bade him cry, with sound of trumpet, all
The hard condition; but that she would loose
The people: therefore, as they loved her well,
From then till noon no foot should pace the street,
No eye look down, she passing; but that all
Should keep within, door shut, and window barr'd.
Then fled she to her inmost bower, and there
Unclasp'd the wedded eagles of her belt,
The grim Earl's gift; but ever at a breath
She linger'd, looking like a summer moon
Half-dipt in cloud: anon she shook her head,
And shower'd the rippled ringlets to her knee;
Unclad herself in haste; down the stair
Stole on; and, like a creeping sunbeam, slid

From pillar unto pillar, until she reach'd
The Gateway, there she found her palfrey trapt
In purple blazon'd with armorial gold.
Then se rode forth, clothed on with chastity:
The deep air listen'd round her as she rode,
And all the low wind hardly breathed for fear.
The little wide-mouth'd heads upon the spout
Had cunning eyes to see: the barking car
Made her cheek flame; her palfrey's foot-fall shot
Light horrors thro' her pulses; the blind walls
Were full of chinks and holes; and overhead
Fantastic gables, crowding, stared: but she
Not less thro' all bore up, till, last, she saw
The white-flower'd elder-thicket from the field,
Gleam thro' the Gothic archway in the wall.
Then shade rode back, clothed on with chastity;
And one low churl, compact of thankless earth,
The fatal byword of all years to come,
Boring a little auger-hole in fear,
Peep'd -- but his eyes, before they had their will,
Were shrivel'd into darkness in his head,

And dropt before him. So the Powers, who wait

On noble deeds, cancel'd a sense misused;
And she, that knew not, pass'd: and all at once,
With twelve great shocks of sound, the shameless noon
Was clash'd and hammer'd from a hundred towers.
One after one: but even then she gain'd
Her bower; whence reissuing, robed and crown'd,
To meet her lord, she took the tax away
And built herself an everlasting name.

The Blind Boy - Colley Cibber

O SAY what is that thing call'd Light,
Which I must ne'er enjoy;
What are the blessings of the sight,
O tell your poor blind boy!

You talk of wondrous things you see,
You say the sun shines bright;
I feel him warm, but how can he
Or make it day or night?

My day or night myself I make
Whene'er I sleep or play;
And could I ever keep awake
With me 'twere always day.

With heavy sighs I often hear
You mourn my hapless woe;
But sure with patience I can bear
A loss I ne'er can know.

Then let not what I cannot have
My cheer of mind destory:
Whilst thus I sing, I am a king,
Although a poor blind boy.

The Litany of Reconciliation

All have sinned and fallen short of the glory of God.

The hatred which divides nation from nations.
Race from race, class from class.
> *Father, forgive.*

The covetous desires of people and nations
To possess what is not their own.
> *Father, forgive.*

The greed which exploits the work of human
Hands and lays waste the earth.
> *Father, forgive.*

Our envy of the welfare and happiness
Of others,
> *Father, forgive.*

Our indifference to the plight of the imprisoned.

The homeless, the refugee.
> *Father, forgive.*

The lust which dishonours the bodies
Of men, women and children.
> *Father, forgive.*

*The pride which leads us to trust in ourselves
And not in God.*
                    Father, forgive.

Be kind to one another, tender hearted, forgiving one another, as God in Christ forgave you.

Note: **Coventry Cathedral**

Reconciliation has been a mark of Coventry Cathedral's ministry since long before the medieval building was destroyed by enemy action in November 1940. It was, however, that tragedy and the community's response under the leadership of Provost Dick Howard which led-to the Christian message of peace, forgiveness and reconciliation (both with God and with our human enemies) becoming the Cathedral's distinctive heartbeat.

Just six weeks after the bombing, Provost Howard said on national radio that, once the war was over, his vision was to work with those who had been enemies "to build a kinder, more Christ-Child-like world." He had the phrase Father forgive inscribed on the wall of the ruined Cathedral, where it can still be seen today. These words echo the prayer of Jesus as he hung dying on the cross: "Father, forgive them, for they do not know what they are doing."

The simple prayer Father forgive acknowledges our need to receive forgiveness from God for ourselves as well as ask it for others.

18 years later, Canon Joseph Poole, the first Precentor of the new Cathedral, wrote out Litany of Reconciliation. Loosely based on the seven deadly sins (anger, gluttony, greed, envy, sloth, lust and pride) it is a confession of humanity's failings. Drawing on different elements of Christian tradition, its message and the values it evokes to deal with human failure are universal and timeless. The new Cathedral was consecrated in 1962. It stands alongside the ruins, as an icon of God's power at work in his world to reconcile and renew. The Litany of Reconciliation is said at 12 noon each weekday. Many other associated centres of reconciliation around the world join us in using this prayer, especially at mid-day on Fridays.

Who? - Charles Causley

Who is that child I see wandering, wandering
Down by the side of the quivering stream?
Why does he seem not to hear, though I call him?
Where does he come from, and what is his name?

Why do I see him at sunrise and sunset
Talking, in old-fashioned clothes, the same track?
Why, when he walks, does he cast not a shadow
Though the sun rises and falls at his back?

Why does the dust lie so thick on the hedgerow
By the great field where a horse pulls the plough?
Why do I see only meadows, where houses
Stand in a line by the riverside now?

Why does he move like a wraith by the water,
Soft as the thistledown on the breeze blown?
When I draw near him so that I may hear him,
Why does he say that his name is my own?

I Remember, I Remember - Thomas Hood

I Remember, I Remember

I remember, I remember
The house where I was born,
The little window where the sun
Came peeping in at morn;
He never came a wink too soon
Nor brought too long a day;
But now, I often wish the night
Had borne my breath away.

I remember, I remember
The roses red and white,
The violets and the lily cups--
Those flowers made of light!
The lilacs where the robin built,
And where my brother set
The laburnum on his birthday,--
The tree is living yet!

I remember, I remember
Where I was used to swing,
And thought the air must rush as fress
To swallows on the wing;
My spirit flew in feathers then
That is so heavy now,
The summer pools could hardly cool
The fever on my brow.

I remember, I remember
The fir-trees dark and high;
I used to think their slender tops
Were close against the sky;
It was a childish ignorance,
But now 'tis little joy
To know I'm farther off from Heaven
Than when I was a boy.

Jerusalem ("And did those feet in ancient time") - William Blake

And did those feet in ancient time
Walk upon England's mountains green?
And was the holy Lamb of God
On England's pleasant pastures seen!

And did the Countenance Divine
Shine forth upon our clouded hills?
And was Jerusalem builded here,
Among these dark Satanic Mills?

Bring me my Bow of burning gold:
Bring me my arrows of desire:
Bring me my Spear: O clouds unfold!
Bring me my Chariot of fire.

I will not cease from mental fight,
Nor shall my sword sleep in my hand
Till we have built Jerusalem
In England's green and pleasant land.

Acknowledgements

Finally – and you've done very well if you got this far with me – I'd like to thank my friends and my children who kindly contributed to the formation and fruition of this project. And a big, big thank you to my forever young family members who are each woven as bright and unique features in my life's rich tapestry!

Printed in Great Britain
by Amazon